12 STORIES OF REAL PEOPLE WHO DISCOVERED

THE LIFE-CHANGING POWER OF GRACE

EVERYBODY NEEDS TO FORGIVE SOMEBODY

NEW AND EXPANDED THIRD EDITION

Allen R. Hunt

Everybody Needs to Forgive Somebody
New and Expanded Third Edition

First edition published as *Where Real Life and Faith Come Together*
Copyright © 2006 Allen Hunt
Second edition copyright © 2012 Allen R. Hunt

To protect the privacy of certain individuals, names
and identifying circumstances have been modified.

Design: Dan Donohue
Interior: Finer Points Productions

ISBN 978-1-942611-82-0 (hardcover)
ISBN 978-1-942611-83-7 (softcover)

Library of Congress Cataloging-in-Publication Data
Names: Hunt, Allen Rhea, 1964- author.
Title: Everybody needs to forgive somebody : 12 stories of real people who
discovered the life-changing power of grace / Allen R. Hunt.
Description: New, expanded third edition | North Palm Beach, Florida :
Beacon Publishing, Inc., [2016]
Identifiers: LCCN 2016027713| ISBN 9781942611820 (hardcover : alk. paper) |
ISBN 9781942611837 (softcover : alk. paper) | ISBN 9781942611844 (ebook)
Subjects: LCSH: Forgiveness--Religious aspects--Christianity. | Forgiveness
of sin. | Grace (Theology) | Catholic Church--Doctrines.
Classification: LCC BV4647.F55 H85 2016 | DDC 241/.4—dc23
LC record available at https://lccn.loc.gov/2016027713

For more information on this title or other books and CDs available through the
Dynamic Catholic Book Program, please visit www.DynamicCatholic.com.

The Dynamic Catholic Institute
5081 Olympic Blvd • Erlanger • Kentucky • 41018
Phone: 1–859–980–7900
Email: info@DynamicCatholic.com

Printed in the United States of America

To Anita, a world-class forgiver and best friend

| CONTENTS |

PART 1: RECEIVING FORGIVENESS

*Experiencing God and forgiving yourself, which may
be the most difficult forgiveness of all*

PART 2: DECIDING TO FORGIVE

*No great journey ever started with anything
less than a decision to begin.*

PART 3: SHARING FORGIVENESS

The law of the harvest is simple: If you want more of something in your life, share it generously with others.

Imagine

Imagine you meet a soldier walking down the street in the first century. You see the sparkle in his eyes as he meets you. Joy radiates off his face as if he has won the lottery. You ask him why.

He shares that his work today started out in an ordinary way. He had no way of knowing that his day would turn and become special, a veritable red-letter day, a day to be celebrated. When the events unfolded, the soldier could barely contain his joy. Today he won a new coat.

The soldier has just been looking for someone to tell the story to, to recount his remarkable good fortune and to show off his new coat. First, he stopped by the office to clock out for the day. He proudly turned and primped for his coworkers and the ladies who operated the home office. "Check it out! I am styling today. Get a load of this coat! I won it. Can you believe it?" The soldier wanted everyone to see the spoils of his victory that day. The women at the office marveled at the beauty of his fine new coat.

After leaving the office to make his way home, the soldier just had to stop by the tavern to show it to his buddies. He'd grab some wine and show off his new coat. This thing was special, and the soldier wanted to brag. "Check out this new coat I got today. Can you believe it? Look at the fabric. This is some coat!" His friends smiled, laughed, and patted him on the back. What a fine day indeed.

The soldier's enthusiasm bubbled over as he walked into his house. He knew his wife was not going to believe this one . . . a new coat, and such a finely crafted one at that. For soldiers, days like this were few and far between. "Honey, check it out. What do you think? Not a seam on this beauty. Can you believe that I won this at work?"

"That is a fine coat," she replied. "How'd you get it?"

"Well, it started like a regular day at work," he said. "Me and the fellows were out on the hill like we always are. I was minding my cross; Bart and Laz, they were minding theirs. I had a fellow up on mine who the crowd really hated for some reason. They yelled at him. They spat at him. They cussed, they mocked, and they even poked him with sticks. One guy went right up to the guy on my cross and stuck some vinegar on a sponge and stabbed it around his mouth. I mean, they really could not stand this guy. And the thing is, this guy hanging on my cross had a really nice coat. This beauty—I mean, look at it! So me and the boys decided to cast lots for this coat. Not a bad coat for an old Jew. We cast lots, and I won. Can you believe it? It is such a beauty. Everybody says so. Never seen any coat like it before."

Imagine you meet that soldier on the street, and he shares this story. Surely you walk away wondering many things.

Why do you wonder? Because when you think about it, it really is remarkable, isn't it? Jesus died hanging on the cross, and as they cast lots for His garments, He looked down at the soldier you just met and said, "Father, forgive them, for they don't know what they're doing." Jesus gazed into the eyes of this soldier, who gleefully looked forward to showing off his new coat. Then, He forgave him.

As He undergoes an excruciating death, and is subjected to humiliation by the crowd, Jesus actually pauses and offers forgiveness. Astonishing. He stares into the eyes of evil, darkness, and death, and rather than cowering or cursing or complaining about the pain, Jesus unlocks the door of forgiveness right there in front of everyone. Wow.

In fact, when you read the Gospels, this much is clear: Jesus seizes this forgiveness thing, and He just won't let it go. Everywhere Jesus goes, He either teaches about forgiveness or He offers it to someone. Zacchaeus. Peter. The woman at the well. The woman caught in adultery. When Jesus teaches His followers to pray, He tells them to ask for forgiveness and for the strength to forgive other people.

Every place you open the Gospels, Jesus is sounding the bugle of forgiveness. The truth is obvious: Jesus, very simply, is all about forgiveness. So much so that His first sermon is just one word, "Repent!" as He makes it plain that we need forgiveness. And His last words are uttered to the Father from the cross on behalf of the soldiers below. "Father, forgive them, for they know not what they do." In other words, forgiveness is literally the first and last message in Jesus' entire ministry. That alone teaches us how very important forgiveness is to our God. And how important it should be to us.

Forgiveness will unleash a power in your life that is underrated and often ignored. Frankly, that power is life-changing. It is underrated mainly because it is underused. We fail to capture the power of forgiveness because we are afraid of it, because we have grown comfortable in our familiar wounds, or because we are sinfully stubborn. But the power is there waiting for us. That is why I have written this little book. Because everybody needs to forgive somebody. And Jesus shows us how.

The Weight Was Not Only Holding Me Back, It Was Breaking My Back

Locked out. I was just ten years old, away at baseball camp for the first time in my life. I was the youngest participant in the camp at Clemson University, and on my own for the first time in my short life. So when I found myself locked out of my room, I had no idea what to do. My roommate was gone, not that he would have done much. When he found out about my predicament later, he did not care to help provide a solution.

So there I stood in the hallway, a ten-year-old boy wrapped in a towel, trying to return from the shower. Alone, outside the dorm room containing all my worldly possessions, including my prized baseball glove, cleats, and hat, all of which I needed quickly in order to join the other boys on the field.

As a ten-year-old, a state away from Mom and Dad for the first time, I was unnerved by the situation. Humiliated and embarrassed, I frantically went door-to-door in the hall trying to find someone who could help me as I stood hopelessly on the other side of a door that could lead me to where I wanted to be. After much searching, I located a coach who could at least give me clothes and gear to use that day until we found a solution, even if he could not provide a key.

The situation ultimately worked out, but the staff learned from my predicament that little boys are likely to lose keys. When we returned to camp the next summer, all keys were handed out on lanyards so that each boy could wear his key around his neck. That way, every camper held the key and would not find himself locked away from his most valuable belongings or from his dorm room home. I loved that lanyard! It was liberating to know you carried the key with you at all times.

As you will soon discover, Millie made an awful mistake and desperately wanted to come home. But she did not have the key. Peter desperately needed a new path forward out of his prison of failures. But to access that path, he needed a key, something that he did not realize he could possess.

We grow comfortable in the prison cell of our own wounds, mistakes, or failures. But the right key unlocks the closed door. As the key turns the catch or bolt to unlock, it opens the way to a new path.

Perhaps inspired by Psalm 90, I like to call God "home." That is an old Jewish name for God. Home. After all, He is our dwelling place. He is our home. You and I were made by Him and for Him. Home.

You will only really ever feel at home when you are in and

with Him. Most of us are looking to go home. When we are honest, way down deep, we know we are not exactly where we need to be. We feel a little out of place in this world. We know God has more in store and in mind for us, but we do not know how to get there. We think about it. We pray about it. We may even work at it, but we often fail to make any progress toward the home that God has created for us.

That is because we fail to realize that we carry the key. That key is forgiveness. And through faith in Jesus Christ, we are carrying that key with us all the time. Too often, our spiritual lives are blocked and our relationship with God impeded, by the weight of our past failures, mistakes, and disappointments, or by the pain we have endured at the hands of others or even caused others. And somehow we are not able to let go of that weight and pain in order to move forward. We are locked in a prison cell of our past and the wounds we have accumulated.

Forgiveness is hard. Perhaps that is why it is underrated. You and I find forgiveness hard because we are stubborn. Rather than stepping out to healing, we often prefer to sit and feed off our wounds because they are familiar and comfortable. It is easier to do nothing. Maybe we struggle with forgiveness because we are lazy or because we are afraid. But understand this: Forgiveness will transform you and your relationships once you release its power into your life. You will find a new and higher level of living and of relationships. *Forgiveness* is the most powerful word in the English language.

I know because I come from a long line of grudge holders.

In my family, we have a remarkable ability to remember every wrong ever done to us, when it was done, and by whom. We keep an internal list of all the wrongs, a spiritual scorecard to be carried around in our minds at all times. And we occasionally like to trot out that list and chew on it a little longer, as if that will satisfy our souls or make us feel more right.

Grudge holding is not one of our most attractive traits. For years, I carried around with me all the people who had hurt me or disappointed me, like a wheelbarrow full of grudges, resentments, and wrongs to be righted. In fact, I know a man who carries a duffel bag filled with notebooks that contain all the wrongs ever done to him. He has each wrong carefully detailed and organized so he can remember them all and share them with anyone who asks. He carries this duffel bag with him everywhere he goes, even when he leaves work and goes to lunch. Those wrongs and those hurts are always with him. Grudge holding gets heavy.

Like this man's duffel bag, my wheelbarrow of grudges went with me everywhere I went, as if I were some kind of supernatural scorekeeper who could track all the wrongs done to me and remember them in case they were needed at a moment's notice. Hours were spent punishing people in my mind, as if that were somehow producing good fruit. Over time, as that list got longer and longer (meanwhile, by the way, I failed ever to notice the harm and hurt I had caused others because I was too preoccupied with the harm done to me), the weight became too great, so great that it was no longer able to be carried. I needed a full-time job just to keep up with all the hurts I was feeling and remembering. The weight was not only holding me back; it was breaking my back.

That is when I was forced to find the key. A key to let me out of the prison cell of past hurt and wrongs so that I could live in the present and move toward the future. I discovered that the key is forgiveness.

Once found, forgiveness frees. It liberates you from feverishly keeping score and remembering wrongs. It propels you into a new, higher way of living. A life of grace. A life of second chances. A life of seeing the possibilities for people and yourself rather than being debilitated in the swampy muck of what has been. A life in which perfectionism is replaced with joy. A life in which you do not have to carry other people's wrongs or be trapped in the prison of your own.

In the years since, I have become a student of forgiveness, discovering and focusing on people who surpass me in this key that helps us unlock our way home, the key that opens the path to becoming the-best-version-of-yourself.

Thus, this little book of forgiveness shares twelve real stories of forgiveness, from twelve people who have inspired me and who I hope will inspire you. At times, I have changed their names or circumstances to preserve their identities. These twelve real-life examples reveal how God forgives you, how you can learn to forgive someone else, and how you can learn to forgive yourself. My goal is not only to inspire you to forgiveness but to teach you how to experience its power in your own life. My prayer is that these stories will do just that for you. Because everybody needs to forgive somebody.

At the end of each chapter, you will find two questions for discussion to help you grow in and experience forgiveness. You will also find a recommended simple step to take after reading each chapter to help you grow one step toward becoming the-best-version-of-yourself. Forgiveness provides the key to your journey home.

PART 1

RECEIVING FORGIVENESS

Experiencing God and forgiving yourself, which may be the most difficult forgiveness of all

Opening the Way
Home: Millie

"I could see it in his face. I could see it in his eyes."

Millie had made an awful mistake, and she wanted to come home. She desired no more, and she could accept no less.

Married at age eighteen, Millie grew restless ten years later. With three kids to care for, and all the weight of adulthood bearing down on her shoulders, she soon found excitement in the arms of another man. For four months, she met this man clandestinely, and their passionate love affair gripped her entire life, both body and spirit.

After four months of meeting her lover in motels and parked cars, Millie left her husband and three children. She moved in with her paramour. They set up house in the same town, just a few miles away from her husband and kids. Millie's husband was devastated, but he refused to give up on her, their vows, and their family. He wrote her notes. He left her messages. On one occasion, he physically picked her up and took her to church to meet with their pastor. But Millie rejected all of his efforts, even going as far as telling the pastor, "I don't need you. I don't want this. I am finished with all of you."

For nearly a year, Millie reveled in her newfound freedom. No kids. No responsibilities. Just the passion and thrill of being in love with someone new. Or so she thought.

On a Wednesday morning, Millie woke up, in more ways than one. That morning, reality sank in. Millie's mind focused, and she thought, "What in the world have I done?" She knew. She was making the biggest mistake of her life. All the decisions of the past year collapsed around her. She had taken a man who loved her unconditionally, and the children they had created together, and ditched that on the side of the road like a used cigarette butt. The crushing wave of what she had chosen washed over her. And she decided, "I am going home."

Millie had no expectation that her husband would forgive her. She hoped he would at least welcome her. She merely wanted to come home. That was all. To be back in the orbit where she belonged. Whether she could set things right or not did not matter, because at least she would be home.

Millie pulled into the driveway and went to the front door. She heard the kids playing in the backyard and stood there on the doorstep for a very long time. It was Wednesday night, right before her husband and children would leave to attend church. After what felt like a decade, Millie knocked on the door. Her husband opened the front door and she could not look up at him. She was shaking and ashamed.

Her husband took the first step. He placed his hands on Millie's face and held her chin up. Looking into her face, he said, "Welcome home."

She responded, "I wanna come home."

And he pulled her small body to him, and that was it.

They prayed. Millie cried. He cried. They went to church that night. And their pastor, whom Millie had verbally dismissed and rejected those months before, threw open his arms and said, "Welcome home, Millie. I'm so glad you're here."

Those were only the first welcomes Millie received. Open arms soon came from her parents-in-law, as well as from other members of the church.

A week later, Millie discovered that she was pregnant. The news meant one obvious thing: She was carrying the child of her lover. Adultery. Illegitimate child. Husband. Three children depending on her. Needless to say, Millie was broken by the news. The gravity of her mistake crushed her world. One week home, one week of moving toward making things right, and now this. An unexpected and fully unwanted pregnancy with a child who could be a permanent reminder of the biggest mistake Millie had ever made and the very real and deep pain she had inflicted on her family. She knew what she wanted to do: end the pregnancy.

That evening, Millie broke the news to her husband.

Like he had done on the doorstep of their home a week before, he looked her in the eye and said, "This is going to be all right." Millie shared that she did not believe that she could go through with the pregnancy. The pain of the living reminder of her adultery was simply too great to bear. He told her that they would make something wonderful from the pain and raise the baby together.

Fortunately, the paramour did not want anything to do with the child, and Millie and her husband now have another lovely daughter. Her in-laws and closest friends, the handful of people who knew the complete story, welcomed the baby just as they had welcomed Millie home upon her return.

Some of the people in town know, and they ask Millie's husband, "How could you have taken her back? How could you have forgiven her?" He replies the same way each time: "You know, with all that Christ did to forgive me, how could I look at my wife, the woman He gave me to love, and say, 'You know, you've done something so horrible that I can't forgive you'?"

Her husband's generous forgiveness brought Millie home again, this time to stay. His forgiveness brought a baby from death to life, a full-time mother back to her children, his soul mate back to him, and a future to everyone involved. Through forgiveness, Millie's husband created a future of memories that will include grandchildren not yet born and mountaintops not yet reached.

For Millie, the harder part has been to forgive herself. That has taken a few years.

In her words, as she shared with me on my radio show, "It's something that I still struggle with. A few months into the relationship with the other man, I felt I couldn't go back home. I felt like I had gone so far beyond, I'd done too much, and I couldn't go back. I was too bad. I didn't deserve my husband, and the whole time he had made it known that he was waiting for me. He had left me messages. He had left me notes, saying, 'I'm not giving up on us. This is not where you belong and this is not who you are.' It was just so overwhelming."

For Millie, it became a perfect picture of who God is.

When did she feel forgiven by her husband? "The moment I showed up on the doorstep and said, 'I want to come home.' It was instantaneous. I knew it. I could see it in his face. I could see it in his eyes."

Millie assumed it would take a long time to build up trust and to do all of the repair work on her relationship. "I felt like it was going to be a long road, and it really wasn't. From the beginning, I would call him if I thought I was going to be late at work, and I would let him know where I was. But I never felt doubted, and he never threw it up in my face. There was never any of that. The hard part was forgiving myself."

When did she feel forgiven by God? "I knew. I knew when I asked. I think because of him. I knew when I went home. I saw that grace. I saw that mercy. It only comes from God. As humans, we do not come by that naturally. I don't think I could do that either. It's horrible to say now, but if the situation were reversed, I do not think I could do that. I don't think I have that in me. It was so devastating, and it was the most horrible, horrible thing. But my husband is now the baby's father. Yes. He is."

Millie found herself locked out of her own life, imprisoned by the tragedy of her decisions. Only forgiveness could provide the key out of that dark prison of pain. Everybody needs to forgive somebody. While a husband needed to forgive his wife, Millie also needed to forgive herself. Her husband's forgiveness, inspired by the forgiveness of God, opened the door and a path to a restored relationship and a unified future together as a family. His forgiveness did not make him forget Millie's mistake; his forgiveness allowed him to move past it.

| | |

QUESTIONS FOR DISCUSSION

1. Have you ever done something so painful that you find it impossible to forgive yourself? In what part of your life do you feel trapped?
2. Are you embarrassed by a mistake you made? Millie came home. What does it mean to you to "come home"? What would it take to get there?

REAL LIFE HELP 1

Create a forgiveness journal. Begin to list the names of people you have hurt and need to ask for forgiveness. On the next page, you can list people who have hurt you whom you need to forgive. This is not a grudge list. It is a forgiveness list. Spend a moment each day writing down the areas of your life in which you need forgiveness to spring forth. Keeping a journal will also help center your soul each day around the idea of forgiveness so that you can make progress. This journal will also come in handy as you make your way through this book and learn what to do with the items you list in your journal.

Begin your forgiveness journal now by filling in the lines below.

Those I need to ask for forgiveness

_____   _____

_____   _____

_____   _____

Those I need to forgive

_____   _____

_____   _____

_____   _____

2

The Most Successful Failure of All Time: Peter

When Jesus calls you Satan, now that is a bad day.

Can you imagine how Peter must have felt? Once the proud leader of the disciples of Jesus, he surely must have been reduced to a huddled pile of human rubble. After all, he had not once but three times denied even knowing Jesus after proudly boasting at the Last Supper that he was willing to go to the death with Him. More embarrassingly, the Sacred Scriptures show Peter as MIA at the cross as Jesus died. He was nowhere to be found. A coward, Peter likely had hidden from the scene out of fear for his own life. Moreover, he had even fallen asleep three times while Jesus prayed in the Garden of Gethsemane, in spite of the fact that Jesus' only instructions to him were to stay awake.

What does it feel like to know you have failed on such a grand scale? You were the leader, yet you denied the Lord. You were the go-to guy, yet you failed to carry out Jesus' instructions to stay awake. You were the chosen head, yet you failed to show up at the most crucial moment in the life of Jesus, at the cross.

Surely Peter felt humiliated, perhaps more so than any other human in history. It must have been difficult even to go out in public or to face his fellow disciples in the wake of such epic failure.

In a sense, Peter found himself locked in the prison of his own failure and disappointment. Dejected. Hangdog. The weight of his mistakes would have felt like he was carrying a boulder on his back as he sought to scale Everest. Peter likely felt there was no way through the locked door he found himself behind.

And yet when the day of Pentecost dawned in Jerusalem, there Peter stood preaching to the masses. The Holy Spirit descended like tongues ablaze, Peter proclaimed, and three thousand people came to believe. Peter, aided by the Holy Spirit, birthed the Church that day.

How does that kind of transformation occur? From huddled human rubble of failure to bold, triumphant leader and proclaimer of the Truth? What is the catalyst for that?

The truth is plain: Peter, the tragic denier and coward, somehow morphed into the most successful failure of all time. He became Peter, the rock of the Church. He grew into St. Peter. He emerged as the first pope. Peter finished as inspiration for the faith. From zero to hero. How does that happen?

What was Jesus thinking? No human resources office of any company on earth would ever hire Peter. In fact, they probably would not even give him a second thought. His personality tests and résumé show little of merit. Yet Jesus chose him and said, "You are Peter, and on this rock, I will build my Church."

Jesus clearly saw something in Peter that no one else did. Because Peter's shortcomings were legion and legendary.

Peter was shortsighted, myopic. When Jesus took Peter, James, and John up on the mountain and was transfigured before them, Peter dreamed up the bright idea of building cabins there. He wanted to stay on top of that mountain with his close friends, and with Jesus, Elijah, and Moses. Peter had no sense of Jesus' larger mission and purpose beyond that mountain. Myopic.

Peter was self-important. When Jesus and the disciples were traveling, families brought little children to Jesus, hoping that He would touch or speak to the little ones. Peter and the disciples tried to shoo all the children away. They saw the kids as a distraction. They wanted Jesus to themselves, for the grown-ups. And Jesus corrected them: "Let the little children come; for to them belongs the Kingdom of God." Self-important was Peter.

Peter was thick. When Jesus told His followers to be prepared, that He would be arrested, convicted, crucified, and raised, Peter said, "No way! That'll never happen to you, Jesus." Peter thought he understood Jesus and God better than Jesus Himself. And Jesus rebuked Peter: "Get behind me, Satan. You have your mind set on earthly things rather than on heavenly things."

That has to be one of the worst days ever. When Jesus calls you Satan, now that is a bad day. But it happened to Peter. Thick.

Peter had a short fuse. He was hotheaded. When the soldiers came with Judas to arrest Jesus, Peter took a sword and lopped off a soldier's ear, again earning the disapproval of Jesus. Fiery fuse.

So how in the world did this Peter become the rock of the Church, St. Peter?

Because of one defining moment. A moment of extraordinary forgiveness. A turning point in which forgiveness unlocked the door of Peter's past and prepared the way home to God's future. Forgiveness turned the bolt and opened a new path.

This defining moment of Peter's life gives us insight into the very heart of God. A God who sees more in us than we see in ourselves. A God who is willing to forget the past and invite us into a bold, divine future. All by issuing a single power, the one most powerful word in the English language and the defining word of the Christian faith: *forgiveness.*

Here is that moment in Peter's life. When Jesus returns to His disciples in His resurrected form, Peter and some of the disciples have been out fishing and are having a fish fry on the shore of the lake. When Jesus returns, He calls Peter over to the side. It is hard, perhaps even impossible, to imagine how Peter felt as he made his way over to Jesus. A walk of shame.

With all the memories of his failures and cowardice still bouncing in his cranium, Peter stands before Jesus, his Lord.

You remember the conversation—it went something like this:

"Peter, do you love me?"

"Yes, Lord, you know that I love you."

"Feed my lambs."

A second time.

"Peter, do you love me?"

"Yes, Lord, you know that I love you."

"Tend my sheep."

And again. A third time. Just as Peter fell asleep three times at the garden, and denied Jesus three times, now Jesus three times looks beyond the past and offers Peter a future.

"Peter, do you love me?"

"Yes, Lord, you know that I love you."

"Feed my sheep."

Three sleep failures in the garden. Three denials by Peter. Yet here Jesus offers three forgivenesses. He does not throw Peter's failures into his face. No, Jesus looks into Peter's eyes, and rather than dredging up the failures, He extends three offers of a bold, divine future. This is Jesus' grace-filled way of saying, "I chose you in the first place, and I meant what I said. I know your past, but I am offering you a future."

Peter stepped into that promise. He received that forgiveness and moved forward with courage and strength, so much so that when you visit Rome today, if you make a reservation well in advance, you can be included in a tour beneath the Vatican. The guide will take you to an archaeological dig taking place beneath St. Peter's Basilica. As you descend beneath the city, you will find yourself on a first-century street, walking among the ruins of ancient Rome. Your steps will take you to a grave site, a tomb, in a first-century cemetery. And the guide's finger will point you to the tomb of St. Peter himself, buried deep beneath the Vatican.

As you gaze at the tomb, you will look up, and as you do, your eyes will see small slits in the layers of the structure that rise above you from the ground of the first century all the way up to the twenty-first century. As you peer through the darkness up to the light several stories above, you will realize that you are standing directly beneath the altar of St. Peter's Basilica, the mother ship of the Church on earth. The altar of St. Peter's, the liturgical centerpiece of the universal Church, rests directly above the tomb of St. Peter himself.

And then the words will come ringing back to your ears: "You are Peter. And on this rock, I will build my Church." He did just that.

Jesus meant it. He showed Peter the future, and He took him there. Peter became the-best-version-of-himself, St. Peter.

How did He do it? How did Jesus move past Peter's obvious failures and shortcomings? In the same way, He will move past yours. Everybody needs to forgive somebody. Peter needed to forgive himself, and Jesus showed him how. Forgiveness: Jesus gave it, and Peter embraced it.

St. Peter's tomb lies directly beneath the centerpiece of worship for the one, holy, catholic, and apostolic Church because Peter experienced the very centerpiece of faith itself, the first and last word of Jesus. Forgiveness.

Forgiveness unleashes the great force of transformation in your life. Forgiveness flows directly from the heart of God and into yours. That force frees you from the wounds and bondage of the past, from harm you have suffered as well as from harm you have caused. And it sets you free to move forward more strongly into the bold, divine future God has in store for you.

As you grow, you will learn to trust in the very heart of God. The same God who came to us in Jesus and helped a fiery fisherman named Peter to become the most successful failure of all time. If He can do that with Peter, just imagine what He can do with you.

| | |

QUESTIONS FOR DISCUSSION

1. When you think of your mistakes and failures, what comes to mind? Divorce? A time when your stubbornness cost you a relationship? Bankruptcy? Job missteps? Inability to complete an important goal? Inadequacy as a parent? Something you wish you hadn't said? Something else?

2. What inspires you most about St. Peter? How is he like you?

REAL LIFE HELP 2

In the following spaces, write your five biggest mistakes, failures, or disappointments. A good place to do this regularly is in your forgiveness journal from the previous chapter. Once you have written these down, take a moment and recite each one aloud, saying this simple prayer following each one:

Lord, have mercy
Christ, have mercy
Lord, have mercy.

_____

_____

_____

_____

_____

3

Welcoming the Gift: Mitch

His eyes opened. His heart softened. And
he knew what needed to happen next.

Mitch never saw it coming. Not at all. It just never occurred to him.

At Dynamic Catholic's Passion and Purpose for Marriage events, we focus on providing helpful and inspiring ways for couples to reenergize their relationships. I enjoy these half-day events because they are filled as much with laughter as with serious moments.

As part of that experience, couples are invited to do a simple fill-in-the-blank exercise.

It goes something like this: The man and woman sit, hold hands, and face each other. The woman goes first, and I invite her to say, "Please forgive me for _____." She should fill in the blank with something simple for which she desires her husband's forgiveness. I instruct him to respond with only these three words: "I forgive you." No more, no less.

Then the spouses switch roles, and the husband fills in the same blank and asks his wife for forgiveness. Again, she responds with just those three words: "I forgive you."

Two days after leading one of these events, I received a phone call from an attendee, Mitch. He called our office and insisted on talking to me. Frankly, I assumed he wanted to complain about something. On the contrary, he eagerly wanted to share what had happened during that simple fill-in-the-blank exchange with his wife. He had assumed this exchange might be helpful for other couples but certainly not for him and his wife.

"I couldn't believe it," he said. "I thought I knew what was going to happen. My wife was going to say something kind of generic that she wanted me to forgive. Next, I'd give her a basic forgiveness like you said, and then we'd switch. But instead, she sat there for a long time in silence. I started getting nervous. Still more silence. Finally she said, 'Please forgive me for being bitter.'"

Over the phone, Mitch's voice got very serious.

"I was taken aback. I had no idea what she was talking about. I didn't know what to say or do, so I said, 'What do you mean? Bitter? About what?'

"My wife continued, 'Two years ago, when we had that fight. Do you remember?'"

Mitch shook his head tentatively, not really recalling what she was describing.

"You know. That night you got up and stormed out of the bedroom. You went downstairs and slept in the guest room in the basement."

A light went on in Mitch's head. He remembered the argument. When he had gotten up out of bed, he had screamed at her, "That's it! I've had enough. I just can't take this life anymore."

She said, "Ever since then, I've wondered if you were going to leave us. I've been anxious. I've been scared that the next fight would be our last. And I've become bitter. Please forgive me."

What Mitch thought had been just a onetime moment of frustration had instead been something completely different for his wife. For her, that argument was a life-changing conversation. He had not given that fight a second thought, while she had been continually reliving it for two years.

Mitch never saw her honesty coming. He thought there was nothing between them at all. Instead, she spoke the truth and revealed the wall of bitterness that had slowly grown to separate them over two years. What Mitch had seen as a small, almost insignificant thing was actually huge in his wife's eyes and in their marriage.

At that moment, God removed the scales that had prevented Mitch from clearly seeing his wife and her deep hurts. His eyes opened. His heart softened. And he knew what needed to happen next.

He quickly forgave her bitterness. And then he promptly apologized for having created it in the first place with his harsh words and cold demeanor.

Forgiveness given; forgiveness received. Mitch had called our office to say thank you because he had never seen it coming, but he was sure glad it had.

Everybody needs to forgive somebody. And sometimes we do not even realize it.

| | |

QUESTIONS FOR DISCUSSION

1. Might there be an area or relationship in your life in which you are blind to hurts and barriers that have grown over the years? Mitch had no idea that his wife was bitter about the words he had shouted two years before. Examine your life for a possible relationship blind spot to see if there could be an area where forgiveness is needed.
2. When Mitch's wife honestly shared the need for forgiveness in their marriage, Mitch welcomed and received her honesty as a gift. Can you think of times in your life when you have heard difficult words or news from someone you love? Did you welcome those words as a gift or did you reject them?

REAL LIFE HELP 3

Make two copies of this prayer attributed to St. Francis of Assisi. Place one in your bathroom to meditate on when you get ready in the morning. Place the other in your forgiveness journal from chapter 1. Use this prayer each day to close your devotion time with God.

Lord, make me an instrument of your peace;
Where there is hatred, let me sow love;
When there is injury, pardon;
Where there is doubt, faith;
Where there is despair, hope;
Where there is darkness, light;
And where there is sadness, joy.

O Divine Master,
Grant that I may not so much seek
To be consoled as to console;
To be understood as to understand;
To be loved as to love;
For it is in giving that we receive;
It is in pardoning that we are pardoned;
And it is in dying that we are born to eternal life.

Freedom from a
Painful Past: Maria

*"The priest told me, 'You really have no
idea how much God loves you.'"*

When you ask Maria about her childhood in Texas, she doesn't know where to begin. That's because the dysfunction of her family cannot be captured in words.

Her father, an alcoholic migrant farm worker, approached his family in only one way: angry, violent, and out of control. The youngest of nine children, Maria watched as each of her older siblings moved out of the house at the first opportunity.

Finally only Maria and her mother remained. They spent most of their days hiding from the rage and violence that filled their home. Maria would hide in a tool shed behind the house as her father exploded, knife in hand, threatening to kill his wife, his daughter, whoever had poured out his liquor.

Maria's mother eventually could endure no more. And one day, when her husband was working in the fields, she took Maria and their handful of belongings and left. They headed north on a bus, trying to find a stable life away from knives and inflamed tempers. Maria's mother found work and rented a trailer not far from Chicago.

Maria knew poverty well. In fact, she wore it every day. Her only two dresses had been sewn by her mother from fabrics found discarded in the trash by others living in the trailer community. Her one pair of shoes came from a box dropped at the dumpster by people in town ridding themselves of items their children had worn out or grown tired of.

Her classmates in Chicago laughed at her wardrobe and asked her if everyone in her parents' home country dressed that way. They teased her for the way she talked, with a combination of a Mexican accent and Texas twang. Even her teachers enjoyed having her stand and speak in front of the class for all to hear and chuckle at.

Maria loved the idea of church. She would walk by just to hear the music coming through the windows and see all the people dressed up in nice clothes and looking so happy and care-free. But when she tried to go to church on her own, the parents there knew her family and its reputation. And the mothers quickly instructed their daughters not to go near someone from such an awful home. Maria learned quickly that rejection awaited her if she ever entered the church again.

The world made it clear to Maria: No one wanted her. Not her father. Not her school. Not even the Church. She was on her own.

Growing into her teenage years, Maria launched out on her own. With no guidance and no help, she began hanging around all the wrong places, doing all the wrong things, and often experiencing the deepest pains this life has to offer. Substance abuse. Nightclubs. Older men. Disappearing for days at a time. Ultimately she found herself in a life filled with adultery, abuse, rape, failed relationships, and scars so deep that only she and God know them all. It was a pain so powerful that no matter how far she ran, the past and her failures simply followed right behind her. The chaos of her childhood had become the chaos of her present.

Eventually Maria met a man, a navy sailor, who seemed a step above the other men she had known. First of all, he had a job with an income, which made Maria feel safe. Second, while far from perfect, he did not abuse her or hit her. So she married him. But she married him mainly because his father hated her.

Maria's father-in-law was an opinionated, self-righteous church person like all the ones who had shunned Maria years before, when she was a little girl. To Maria, it felt good to marry someone knowing that his father and his religion hated every bit of it.

Maria never deeply trusted her husband, never confided in him. She just went through life on her own, making it as best she could. She reared her four children and managed family life as well as she was able, given all the chaos she had known in her own life and family.

But slowly, as the years passed and the children grew, since her husband had always attended Mass, Maria began to attend with him. She didn't really understand all that was going on, but she was drawn to the reverence, the quiet, and the holy sacredness that just seemed to envelop her each time she walked through the door.

Over time, Maria began volunteering to do the dirtiest tasks in the church, things that have to be done in any parish but no one else was willing to do. Scrubbing toilets. Cleaning the kitchen. Pulling weeds. Even repairing the roof.

When the priest asked her why she wanted all those menial roles, she said, "I guess I'm trying to make it up to God. I've got a lot to make up for. I know I can't work my way to heaven, but . . . " And her voice trailed off.

Later, the priest, who became her pastor, asked her whether she knew the grace and forgiveness of God. She replied, "I hope so. I am like the woman at the well. It is just hard for me to believe that Jesus could love even me, knowing all the things in my childhood and in my past."

Eventually, Maria found her way home to the Church. Her first reconciliation nearly consumed her as she recited the long list of pains from her life. But then she was met with the divine mercy of God. It flowed like a waterfall, cascading over her and saturating every fiber of her heart. She found it overwhelming. In her own words, "The priest told me, 'You really have no idea how much God loves you.' He's right. I'm just beginning to discover that. And it's wonderful!"

With the help of her faith, the friendship of two fellow

participants in a support group, and the assistance of a wise, well-trained counselor, Maria learned to release much of the pain of her past. She grew to forgive her father for her deep childhood hurts. She even came to forgive her father-in-law. And she finally was able to forgive herself.

Everybody needs to forgive somebody.

Forgiveness produces healing and a path forward. The key of forgiveness opens the door to a new future. Forgiveness does not forget the violence, the wounds, the wrongs. It moves past them.

Jesus' heart loves first.

Jesus' heart is mercy.

Jesus' heart is to forgive.

His promise is always greater than our past.

Believe it.

Embrace it.

|||

QUESTIONS FOR DISCUSSION

1. Do you carry any childhood hurts? Can you see areas of your life where those pains from the past continue to affect you and your relationships today?

2. Do you think forgiving is the same as forgetting? Does it help to understand that forgiving means moving past rather than forgetting?

REAL LIFE HELP 4

Three Steps Toward Healing and Forgiveness of Pains from the Past

1. Approach those pains from the past with someone else. Seek out a caring, confidential friend, an excellent priest, or a trained counselor. There is strength in the presence of a listening, attentive person. You are not alone. Studies even show that sharing your pain with someone else helps your brain to begin to rewire itself.

2. Consider applying the Stations of the Cross to your own pain. Have someone accompany you as you pray through the Stations of the Cross. Envision the pain of Christ Jesus at each station. Then envision Him being with you in the moments from your past that are painful to you. Feel Him nearby in your pain now. It is powerful to run your feelings through the filter of your faith and the cross of Jesus. Through the Stations of the Cross, let Jesus enter your pain with you and begin the release of that pain, just as He did through His own cross.

3. At times, God will take the pain away in obvious ways. At other times, it will be more of a choice for you, knowing that God is asking you to forgive and understanding that you need to choose forgiveness for your own well-being.

   Just as sharing your pain with a caring person allows you to rewire the brain, imagine how much more powerful healing can be when Jesus is experiencing it with you through the Stations of the Cross.

Let patience be your friend. Healing and forgiveness take time, often a very long time. You have been carrying these memories and hurts for a long time, so it only makes sense that healing will require time too. St. Teresa of Ávila said, "Patience achieves everything." That is true for your healing as well.

PART 2

DECIDING TO FORGIVE

*No great journey ever started with
anything less than a decision to begin.*

There's Gotta Be a Better Way: Bud

"I have to do something different, because what I am doing now is killing me."

In the spring of 1995, Julie Marie Welch was a bright twenty-three-year-old with a promising future. Just 5'1" and 103 pounds, she packed much zest into a small package. After graduating from Marquette University as a foreign language major, Julie had returned to her hometown of Oklahoma City to work for the Social Security Administration. She translated for clients who struggled with English. She attended Mass each morning before work and had recently discovered anew the power of faith in her life. Julie had even met Eric, her fiancé, at a young singles' prayer meeting.

On Wednesday morning, April 19, 1995, Julie went to Mass, and then headed to her office on the first floor of the Alfred P. Murrah Federal Building. Early in the day, she walked out to the waiting area to receive a client. While she was in the corridor on her way back to her office, Timothy McVeigh detonated a bomb that killed her and 167 other people. McVeigh would later claim that his violent act was revenge on the federal government for what he saw as oppressive actions against the Branch Davidian cult in Waco, Texas. He chose that day, the second anniversary of the inferno that had consumed David Koresh and his followers in Waco, to blow up Julie Welch and the other victims of his Murrah Building bombing.

At the time of the explosion, Julie's father, Bud Welch, turned on the television to see a nine-story pile of rubble where the Murrah Building had been. Instantly, he lost hope for his daughter's survival. Ironically, no one in Julie's work area was hurt. If she had returned from the corridor seconds earlier, she would have survived.

I first met Julie's father by phone, and then in person. Bud's deep eyes communicated clearly how much he had loved his daughter. For days after the blast, full of pain and anger, he drove to the site to remember, to reflect, and to wonder where to go from here. The first months of grief were the worst experience of his life. He obsessed about vengeance on McVeigh; his mind envisioned a quick and violent execution. Nothing more, nothing less could satisfy Bud's anger and pain. Or so he thought.

Bud began to self-medicate with alcohol each night from the moment he returned home from work at his Texaco station until he passed out for the night. The pain of Julie's death consumed him. His hangovers grew worse with each passing week. His cigarette habit shot from one to four packs per day. Slowly but surely, Bud Welch was destroying himself. The loss was simply too great.

Finally, in January 1996, Bud drove to the Murrah bomb site again. As he stood across the street and looked at the rubble, his head still aching from the night before, he thought to himself, "I have to do something different, because what I am doing now is killing me. It's not working. There's gotta be a better way." Vengeance had motivated McVeigh's bombing and massacre, and Bud could see where that had led—to a tragic bomb site, a daughter gone forever, and the soul of a broken father swimming in anguish.

Bud slowly began to soften. He changed from wanting McVeigh to be executed to simply wanting him to be tried and convicted—justice, not vengeance. Wanting the death penalty felt too much like revenge to Bud. He began his first steps toward healing by speaking openly against the death penalty to students at colleges and universities. Sharing his story also helped him to deal with the grief of Julie's death. By talking openly, he was able to let out the pain he had been carrying around inside and trying to numb with his addictions. By June 1998, Bud was well on his way to overcoming his dependence on whiskey and cigarettes and was exploring what to do next.

Soon after, Bud received an invitation to meet with Bill McVeigh, Tim's father. A Catholic nun arranged the visit for a time when Bud was already scheduled to speak in the Buffalo, New York, area. Upon pulling up in front of the McVeigh home, with great anxiety, Bud got out of the car and walked up to the house where Tim the terrorist had spent much of his life. The ghosts haunting Bud were almost too much. He stopped, calmed himself, and moved forward. Slowly he entered the yard to meet the man who had reared a son who had grown up to commit the worst act of terror on American soil to that date. At the door, Bud was greeted by Bill, whom Bud had seen only on television shortly after the tragic bombing.

Bud and Bill walked and talked around the McVeighs' garden for thirty minutes. They then went into the house, where Tim's sister, Jennifer, joined them at the table. Their conversation unfolded slowly and nervously, but Bud knew he had made the right decision to meet in person. He could not help but notice a large, eight-by-ten photo of Tim McVeigh hanging on the wall in the kitchen. Sensing that Bill and Jennifer were probably self-conscious about how often he was looking at the photo, Bud suddenly blurted out, "My, what a good-looking kid."

Bill replied, "Bud, can you cry?"

Bud said, "Yes, why?"

Bill shared that he had not cried for years. At that moment, a large tear fell from his eye and rolled down his cheek. They were two fathers together mourning a horrific tragedy in which each had lost a child. As Bud stood to leave, the three of them—Bud, Bill, and Jennifer—embraced. Bud and Bill shook hands. Bud hugged Jennifer once more, and they began to sob together. Bud sobbed more than he ever had before or since as an adult. At that moment, he could see the love of a father in the eyes of Bill McVeigh. Bud's forgiveness had opened the door to reconciliation and healing, a new path forward both for him and for the McVeighs. When Tim McVeigh was executed in 2001, Bud, who already knew the pain of having to bury a child, now shared that same pain of a father's loss with Bill McVeigh.

Everybody needs to forgive somebody. Bud needed not only to forgive Tim McVeigh, he needed to establish a real relationship with McVeigh's father. Bud would even say that he needed to forgive God for allowing this awful tragedy to happen.

In this case, Bud had no choice. Clinging to his pain and desire for vengeance literally was killing him from the inside out. And his journey to forgiveness took five long years after Julie's tragic death. To this day, he still cannot explain how that process works, only that it takes time, patience, and prayer, applying their heart-softening salve slowly but surely to a hurting soul.

Bud still sees pain etched on the faces of those Oklahoma City victims' families who have been unable to forgive. They are trapped in their anguish, and the wound continues to fester deep within. He knows from his own experience there is only one key that can open the door to healing and a new life.

Forgiving does not mean condoning what Timothy McVeigh did. It also does not require Bud to forget Julie, her beauty, and the potential that was snuffed out that day in the bombing. Instead, forgiveness allows Bud to release the pain and poison and move forward to honor Julie with a healthy and meaningful life. He now helps others learn how to forgive. He aids people in discovering new life.

It is often not an easy thing, this forgiveness. But it is a life-saving thing. Without it, anger leads to resentment, which leads to bitterness, which leads, finally, to spiritual death. A flash of anger and regret returns on occasion when Bud sees a young woman who reminds him of Julie, or when he dreams that he has seen Julie alive again, but he then moves forward, knowing that to live in the past is to die. He has made the choice to move past the pain and into the future. Bud Welch has chosen the better way.

| | |

QUESTIONS FOR DISCUSSION

1. What is the most painful hurt you have ever experienced at the hands of another person?
2. When you think of the person who hurt you, which comes to mind first: revenge or release? Why?

REAL LIFE HELP 5

Visualize your deepest hurts and resentments. These resentments may include people who have hurt you, those who have betrayed you, and those who have injured people you love. Envision each hurt as a rock, a time when you were stung by someone's unkind words or harmful actions, and in your mind's eye, slowly place that rock in a bag. Repeat this as often as needed to gather all the hurts and resentments you are carrying within you. Some may be large rocks, big wounds, while others may be smaller pebbles that you still seem to cling to.

In your imagination, place that bag of rocks in the trunk of your car. Get in the car and drive to a nearby lake. See yourself getting out of the car. Now remove the large bag of rocks, lift it over your shoulder, and throw it into the lake. Watch as the bag plunges into the lake and disappears from sight. Feel the release that comes from knowing that those hurts, grudges, and resentments you were carrying are now making their way down to the bottom of the lake.

Get back into your car. Drive away. The weight is gone. The rocks no longer travel with you. You need no longer carry them in your mind or in your soul.

You have left them there, permanently. They are gone.

Releasing the
Poison: Mother

Officer van de Broek did not hear the words of the
hymn. He had fainted, completely overwhelmed.

Officer van de Broek certainly did not merit forgiveness.
Anyone could see that. He had behaved like a depraved
animal. Nevertheless, there he stood, and one woman had his
fate in her hands.

Giving grace to those who deserve vengeance seems un-
just—at least to us humans. We like our grudges. We hold on
to them in hopes of arriving at that day when we can give the
offender his or her comeuppance. That is human. But God is not
human—anything but. Grace provides a breathtaking snapshot
of the heart of God. In forgiving, you experience the radical love
of God, and you can actually feel His heart.

An unnamed South African woman, described by Philip
Yancey in his *Rumors of Another World*, captures this power.

Nelson Mandela taught the world about the power of grace. After he emerged from twenty-seven years in prison and was elected the new president of South Africa, his first act was to invite his jailer to join him on the presidential inauguration platform. Mandela then appointed Archbishop Desmond Tutu to head an official government panel with an intimidating name, the Truth and Reconciliation Commission (TRC), to try to bring the racially fractured nation together. Mandela wanted to defuse the natural human pattern of revenge that he had seen firsthand in prison and in so many countries where one race or tribe had taken control from another.

For two and a half years, South Africans listened to reports of atrocities from the TRC hearings. The TRC rules were simple: If a white policeman or army officer voluntarily faced his accusers, confessed his crime, and fully acknowledged his guilt, he could not be tried and punished for that crime. South African hard-liners grumbled about the obvious injustice of letting criminals go free. Mandela, however, insisted that the country needed healing more than it needed justice. He chose to focus on that radical agenda of healing, a new door that could be opened only with the key of forgiveness. Everybody needs to forgive somebody, and that truth was never more apparent than in South Africa.

At one hearing, a policeman named van de Broek shared how he and other officers had entered a village and shot an eighteen-year-old boy. After the murder, they burned the boy's body, turning it on the fire like a piece of barbecue meat in order to destroy the evidence. Eight years later, van de Broek returned to the same house and this time seized the boy's father. The man's wife was forced to watch as policemen bound her husband on a woodpile, poured gasoline over his body, and ignited it.

The courtroom grew hushed as the elderly woman who had lost first her son and then her husband listened to Officer van de Broek's confession. She was then given a chance to respond.

"What do you want from Mr. van de Broek?" the judge asked. The woman stood. She said she first wanted van de Broek to go to the place where they had burned her husband's body and gather up the dust so she could give him a decent burial. After all, that dust was all she had left of her family. His head down, the policeman nodded in agreement.

Then she added a second request. "Mr. van de Broek took all my family away from me, and I still have a lot of love to give," she said. "Twice a month, I would like for him to come to the ghetto and spend a day with me so I can be a mother to him. And I would like Mr. van de Broek to know that he is forgiven by God, and that I forgive him too. I would like to embrace him so he can know my forgiveness is real."

Spontaneously, some of the observers who were gathered in the courtroom began singing "Amazing Grace" as the elderly woman made her way to the witness stand. Officer van de Broek did not hear the words of the hymn. He had fainted, completely overwhelmed.

Van de Broek had entered the courtroom that day locked in the tiny prison cell of his painful atrocities. Rather than revealing a thirst for vengeance, the widow had extended the key that would unlock a new life: forgiveness.

Everybody needs to forgive somebody. In this case, an entire nation needed to forgive a racially violent past. And one woman needed to forgive a man who had taken away the most beautiful parts of her life. Very simply, she chose to overcome van de Broek's evil act with her own act of love.

Rather than holding on to the poison of those murders, the woman chose to release it. Rather than deflecting the poison of hate back into the face of van de Broek, she reflected love into his heart.

Because of her, everyone in that room, including the man who had crushed her family, was changed by grace.

|||

QUESTIONS FOR DISCUSSION

1. Have you ever known someone who was murdered? Have you been close friends with a family who has suffered the murder of a loved one? How have they handled that violent death? Have they handled it well or are they struggling to deal with the anger?

2. What is the most important lesson for your life from this story from South Africa?

REAL LIFE HELP 6

Seven steps you can take toward a lifestyle of forgiveness

1. First, remember your own need for forgiveness. Admit that you often are not the-best-version-of-yourself. Recognize that God still loves you immeasurably. He does forgive you. You are forgiven; therefore, you too can forgive.

2. Clearly define only one thing that someone has done to you that you know you ought to forgive. Don't try to forgive all people and all wounds at once. Pick one to begin.

3. Pray and ask God to saturate you with His spirit of grace. You cannot forgive on your own; the task is too large. But with God's help, the task becomes small. He is a forgiver and will make you one too.

4. If possible, engage the "offender" in direct, open, and honest communication. Share how you have been hurt, but do not be accusatory. Focus more on yourself and how you feel than on the other person. He or she needs to hear your pain rather than feel a finger of accusation. The goal is healing, not perpetuating the pain. Be compassionate even in confrontation. Say these simple words: "I forgive you." Often, we clutter the conversation with too many words and explanations. Be simple. These words are powerful. Let them stand on their own.

5. Follow up your simple words of forgiveness with some act of reconciliation—perhaps a hug or a handshake, or a meal together. (Remember that there are some instances in

which it is not possible or healthy to engage face-to-face with someone who has hurt you.)

6. To prevent the same hurts from occurring again, keep your lines of communication open, with clear boundaries and guidelines for your relationship. Now that you have been open and honest, your relationship will be more open and honest too. You both are more aware of each other and how the relationship can be easily fractured. That awareness can help you draw healthy boundaries for a healthy relationship. It is also important to know that forgiving someone does not necessarily mean inviting him or her back into your life.

7. Finally, learn to forgive the small things—with your friends, family members, spouse, or coworkers. Be a person of grace. Recognize that you are still prone to making mistakes as you become the-best-version-of-yourself, just as others are. Don't dwell on the small hurts that we all experience daily and, frankly, that we all cause in others. Give the grace you wish to receive. The more grace you give, the more you will receive.

7

Fix Forward: Thomas

"It would have killed me. It would have done more damage to me than good."

You may have never heard of Thomas Doswell. That's because he spent nineteen of the best years of his life in prison for rape. Thomas, a black man, was convicted of the 1986 rape of a forty-eight-year-old white woman at a hospital in Pittsburgh. He was sentenced to thirteen to twenty-six years in prison. When he entered prison, Thomas, the father of two young children, was just twenty-five years old.

During nearly two decades in prison, Thomas Doswell was denied parole four times because he insisted he was innocent. He steadfastly refused to accept responsibility for the rape. Nevertheless, prosecutors opposed any testing of DNA material from the rape victim.

The Innocence Project of the Benjamin N. Cardozo School of Law at Yeshiva University assisted Thomas and his attorney, demanding that the testing be done. In 2005, after years of requests and petitions, one judge finally ordered that the rape-kit evidence be tested for DNA. To the surprise of nearly everyone but Thomas, the results proved that he had been telling the truth all along. The semen taken from the victim was not his. The DNA evidence corroborated Thomas' steadfast denials of guilt. A week later, prosecutors agreed to join his motion to vacate his conviction and sentence, and he was finally released from prison—nineteen long years after entering to serve a sentence for a crime he did not commit.

It is almost impossible to conceive what that conviction did, and what those years wrongfully served in prison felt like, to Thomas Doswell. Nineteen years taken away from his life. Nineteen years of not being able to be a father to his children. Nineteen years of bearing the label "rapist" and the stigma it carries. A good name ruined. How do you recover from that?

The victim and another witness had identified Thomas from a group of photos shown to them by police. At the time, Pittsburgh police marked mug shots of people charged with rape with the letter *R*. Thomas had insisted that the witnesses identified him as the rapist only because that *R* appeared under his picture. Since that time, police no longer mark photos this way. But that change does not alter the fact that Thomas Doswell sat in prison for all those years because of the faulty methods used to pin the crime on him.

Most people in his situation would have grown angry and resentful. Instead, while Thomas was in prison, he looked forward rather than backward. He used the time to become a-better-version-of-himself. He earned a degree, learned to speak Spanish, and mastered seven instruments, including guitar, saxophone, flute, drums, and trumpet.

How did he do it? Faith. "Having the faith I have in Jesus has taught me that I couldn't walk around for twenty years with anger bottled up in me," says Thomas. "It would have killed me. It would have done more damage to me than good."

So, on that fateful day that he had known would come in spite of all opposing forces, Thomas Doswell walked out of prison. On the day of his release, his mother, Olivia, led a crowd of tearful, smiling relatives and friends in chanting, "God is good." Thomas had inspired his family to become better rather than bitter, through faith in a God of redemption.

Thomas forgave the police officer, who he believed had focused on him because he had been acquitted of sexual assault a year earlier. He forgave the rape victim, who had identified him despite clear differences between his appearance and that of the assailant. He even forgave the prosecutors who fought his appeals and tried to stop the DNA testing.

Through faith, Thomas realized that he had no choice but to forgive. The choice was quite clear: He could choose death, by hanging on to the anger and injustices committed against him, or he could choose life. Either way, life would move on, but *how* it moved on was up to him. He could look forward or backward. Backward led to bitterness; forward led to a future. Thomas decided to fix forward because he could not fix backward.

While Thomas was in prison, his two sons grew up. He missed

their parent-teacher conferences, he missed their ball games, and he missed teaching them how to change a tire and catch a ball. Thomas missed his father's funeral, instead weeping as he listened in on the telephone in prison while singing "Amazing Grace."

Nevertheless, Thomas Doswell somehow emerged whole from an awful tragedy that would have broken most mortals. He says, "Despite being away from family and being away from freedom that you had always rightfully deserved to have, God has blessed me and I managed to come through in a positive light."

He can get on with the rest of his life because he knows the power of forgiveness. He faced a choice. And he decided to forgive. Everybody needs to forgive somebody. Thomas Doswell needed to forgive lots of people. And when he did, life opened up before him rather than crumbling around him in the prison cell in which he sat.

| | |

QUESTIONS FOR DISCUSSION

1. Have you ever been falsely accused of something? Perhaps a friend suggested that you had been gossiping about her. Or a business associate implied that you had been less than fair. How did that feel?

2. If you could fix forward, what would you do? If you asked for God's help with that, what specifically would you ask Him to help you with?

REAL LIFE HELP 7

Carry a crucifix in your pocket or in your purse. Holding it in your hand at times throughout the day can be a healing, physical reminder of the forgiveness that flows from above. Rub your fingers gently over the body of Christ crucified. Remember His dying words: "Father, forgive them, for they don't know what they're doing." Experience the grace of knowing that His forgiveness far surpasses yours, and His strength is available to you. In the cross, He releases the past and helps you fix forward.

PART 3

SHARING FORGIVENESS

*The law of the harvest is simple:
If you want more of something in your
life, share it generously with others.*

8

The First Step: Amy

She had taken the first step.

Shortly after becoming a pastor at a new church, I experienced a church clash of such grand proportions that it exploded into the worst conflict in my life and ministry. A disagreement pitted the church leaders against the board of directors of the grade school affiliated with the church. The conflict turned nasty. Then it went public. Because a number of high-profile personalities were involved, the entire city and the press covered the story.

The two sides divided over the future direction of the school. And no one was uninvolved. In a church with more than five thousand members and a school with more than a thousand children, the dispute spilled into the community. Board members, parents, church members, friends, colleagues—everyone chose sides. The tumult was bitter, ugly, and hostile.

As the new pastor on the staff, I walked into the beginnings of this fight with a different set of eyes because I knew so few of the people and so little of the history that had sparked the fire. Because I brought a fresh perspective and a small measure of objectivity as a newcomer, I became the church's chief public spokesperson. More challenging, my job required me to be the primary worker, both behind the scenes and in public meetings, seeking resolution to this toxic situation.

As a result, this conflict placed me before large groups of people in public meetings, often with dozens, sometimes even hundreds of people attending, and a few involving press coverage. My time shifted between meeting with members or leaders, with school parents or faculty, and with the school's board of directors. It is hard to overstate how long and arduous this process became. Meetings, large and small, occurred nearly daily for more than a year. This fight consumed my work as a pastor whether I wanted it to or not. None of these meetings were fun. The experience was much like running a gauntlet of people flailing at you with sharp knives, finishing the run, turning around, and running through it again. Day after day. For more than a year. I still feel the residue of that experience lingering on my skin to this day.

One group in particular was the most painful to deal with: the group of parents who had chosen to oppose the church. My meetings with them were often periods of yelling and anger, followed by scheduling more meetings to do the same. At most of these hostile parents' meetings, I faced one particular mother, whom I will call Amy. She had two children enrolled in the school.

Amy was not only angry and bitter, she was also extraordinarily vocal. She never seemed to have a kind word to say to anyone, least of all me. Amy did not trust me at all. She felt burned by the institution to which she had entrusted her children, so she questioned everything I said and always responded harshly. Her facial expressions and her verbal outbursts intended to draw blood. Unfortunately, this conflict with her dragged on at meeting after meeting for nearly two years, because she was unable to place her children at another school that she preferred. Thus, she and her kids stayed another full year.

Very simply, the experience wore me out, leaving me physically and emotionally drained. Worse still, the trial eroded my willingness and desire to trust people as I had before. Facing an endless barrage of insults, accusations, and lies on a daily basis takes its toll.

That second year, as a group of parents tried to enroll their children at other faith-based schools, became the longest of my life, not only because of Amy, the angry mother, but also because of the tension she and a handful of others created in the halls, offices, and parking lot throughout the school each day. Gossip flourished. Trust broke down. Paranoia set in among the various leaders because no one knew any longer whom they could trust. I did my best to avoid Amy and move on with my life and my new ministry at the church, but instead of dealing with my feelings, I repressed them. I found it increasingly hard to trust other people, and I found less and less joy in my work as a pastor.

Finally, nearly two years after the initial eruptions, this mother and her children moved to another school. I felt relieved that I would no longer have to encounter her or see the anger and bitterness in her eyes, but I could still feel the resentment in my heart. That did not go away.

About a year later, our school and her children's new school played a tennis match. I decided to stop by the courts and watch for a few minutes on the way home, not considering that this mother would be there too. When I got out of my car and began walking toward the tennis courts, my heart sank when I saw Amy walking up to me. My stomach clenched. I braced myself for what was coming. Flashbacks of the previous two years exploded in my head as if I were a soldier reliving Vietnam.

However, instead of the venom I was expecting, Amy reached out her hand and said something like, "Allen, I want to apologize to you. These last few years have been very hard. I realize now that you were telling me the truth. I was very ugly to you, and I apologize. I'm sorry. Please forgive me." I couldn't believe it. I was shocked. I had braced for the worst and never expected what I received.

She had taken the first step. Instead of a clenched fist, Amy had extended an open hand. And in that hand was a key to open the door to let me out of much of the pain and anguish in which I had found myself. Forgiving her had seemed like an impossibility, at least one bridge farther than I could travel. I was too weak. In fact, I had not even been able to muster the energy to try to forgive her. It was just too much.

Everybody needs to forgive somebody. It was clear to me that I needed to forgive Amy. How could I not? But it truly was miraculous—because she took the step I never would have been able to take. Somehow she stepped out and offered me the key to prepare a new path, a path free of the bitterness and poison that had been welling up deep within me.

To be honest, I have never been more surprised in my life than I was at that moment. To be even more honest, I have never felt that free in my life either. It was the most genuine apology I have ever received. It washed over me like a nice shower after a day covered with sand from the beach. And it came from a woman I barely knew outside of the verbal assaults she had directed toward me almost daily for years. Spiritually, I knew I should have prayed for Amy, but I had been unable to do so because of my own pride and unwillingness to deal with the hurt I felt.

Everybody needs to forgive somebody. Usually, the greatest obstacle is one person's unwillingness to take the first step. The mother in this story had courage that I did not. Because of that courage, she and I both experienced new life. Had she not stepped forward, I have no idea how long I would have carried the resentment and hurt inside me. Perhaps I would still have it today. And it would be blocking my ability to live now.

With her remarkable courage and spiritual honesty, Amy taught me much. She handed me the key.

|||

QUESTIONS FOR DISCUSSION

1. Who is the best forgiver in your own life? Why do you think of this person in particular?

2. When has someone taken the first step to forgive you? What did you learn from that experience?

REAL LIFE HELP 8

Make a conscious decision to forgive. Make that decision real by writing "I choose to forgive" right now in the space provided.

_____

Resolve today that you will be a forgiver. Even if you have no idea how, decide to be a forgiver anyway. It is much like learning to ride a bike. You only learn to forgive as you begin doing it. Set your mind and your spirit on forgiveness. Often, the one thing that most prevents moving forward is not being able to decide, "I am choosing to be a forgiver." Choose forgiveness today. A great place to do this is in confession with your priest. Tell him that you want to be a forgiver and ask him to help you.

Make forgiveness a centerpiece of your prayer life each day. It may even change you more than it changes the people around you.

It is the right decision for a lot of reasons, including the basic point that it helps *you* most of all! Believe it or not, those who forgive:

- Benefit from better immune systems and lower blood pressure than those who cannot forgive
- Have better mental health than people who do not forgive

- Have lower amounts of anger, anxiety, and depression than those clinging to old wounds
- Enjoy more satisfying and long-lasting relationships than those who are unable to find a way to forgive

Decide today to be a forgiver. And let the benefits abound!

9

A Process More Than a Moment: Gary

Forgiving is not forgetting.
They are two very different things.

G ary asked, "Why don't you come over and watch the Steel-ers game with me?"

Brooks, Gary's older son, replied, "I can't right now. I'm tak-ing Gregory to get a haircut."

Those words flooded Gary's soul with a tidal wave of regret. His first thought: "I never did that." Hearing that his four-year-old grandson, Gregory, was on his way to get a haircut reminded Gary of how he had missed every haircut of Brooks' childhood. Those little moments—teaching him to play baseball, taking him for a haircut, teaching him to ride a bike—were all sacred moments that Gary had missed. All because of the divorce.

Of course, Gary had not married with the plan to divorce. No one ever does. Wedding days bubble over with hopes and dreams, with possibilities for the future. Divorce days look at the scorched bottom of the saucepan and wonder what happened.

For Gary and his first wife, soon after the arrival of two children, the marriage imploded. There was plenty of blame to go around, but the facts remained the same: Gary was alienated from his own children, and his ex-wife was perfectly happy to limit their time together. Each time Gary would make the drive to the town where his ex-wife and children lived, he would reexperience the pain and rawness. He quickly came to realize why so many men walk away from their children and pasts rather than continuing to step into that kind of pain.

The hurts of the divorce were very real. With a failed marriage, Gary had disappointed himself, his parents, and his faith. He believed he had let God down. Marriage is a sacred vow, and Gary's vows had not survived. Even more painful than that failure was the damage and pain the divorce had inflicted on his two children during their growing-up years. Gary, a man of high standards, had had great expectations for marriage and parenting. He now looked in the mirror and faced the fact that he had not met those expectations.

Professionally, Gary did great. His career soared; he succeeded at every turn and moved his way up to become the CEO of a billion-dollar company. He remarried and did the best he could to father his two children, often from a distance as his job moved him around the world. For the most part, however, Gary was absent. Absent from the haircuts, the baseball practices, and the ballet recitals. Absent from homework and dinner conversations and coaching his kids about life.

Now that his children were grown, they were able to make their own choices and set their own schedules rather than being directed by any parent. As a result, Gary seized the opportunity to create a new kind of life with them. He set a new priority of knowing them well, in a way he had not been able to before, and loving their children, his grandchildren. As a result, he was establishing deeper relationships with them, their spouses, and the newly arriving grandchildren. But every time he was around the kids, looking into their eyes provided a raw reminder of the pain his divorce had created. It was like the divorce was one small pebble dropped into a large pond and continuing to create ripples for years and years—the residual impact of that decision would be felt long after it was made. He could never undo it.

As his new marriage thrived and his relationship with his children improved, Gary also nurtured his faith life. After the divorce, he had taken a long hiatus from God, his faith, and the Church. The seeds of faith had been planted well by his mother when Gary was young, so the potential for growth was still there. He simply had not worked the soil to produce a harvest. Now, as he aged, however, Gary began to return to his faith roots. First he developed a life of prayer. Second, he joined a Bible study. Third, he became a generous giver who used all his resources to invest in God's kingdom rather than in himself.

Through those steps, Gary discovered that forgiveness is often a process more than an instant. This is true particularly when you need to forgive yourself most of all. Everybody needs to forgive somebody, and sometimes that somebody is yourself. In fact, receiving forgiveness from God and forgiving others often come more easily than forgiving yourself. When you realize how much you have hurt the people around you or offended the God who made you, forgiving yourself can be challenging.

Gary made the key decision to place himself in a stream of forgiveness. He listened carefully to the words of Jesus in His parable regarding the servant who wanted forgiveness in his own life but was unwilling to forgive other servants. Gary learned that if he wanted others to forgive him, he needed to place himself in a stream of grace by first forgiving others. And that stream began with allowing God's forgiveness to give him the strength and courage to forgive himself.

In that process of forgiving the people around him, Gary set in motion a wave of grace that eventually boomeranged to saturate his own life. The more Gary forgave, the more grace and forgiveness he received. He took the first step and acknowledged that plenty of mistakes were made in that first marriage. "I will choose to forgive her and to forgive myself. I can do no other. Those mistakes cannot be undone. And I choose not to live continuously in the past." He could not fix backward, but he could fix forward.

And with that wave of forgiving grace, Gary focused on the present rather than on the past. A new resolve set in: "I will be the best father I can be for my kids today. And I will invest thoroughly in my grandchildren." Gary now organizes his life around swim parties and sleepovers, lazy afternoons in the back-yard, and vacations at the beach, all so that he can be as inti-mately involved with his grandchildren as possible. You cannot fix backward, but you can fix forward. And Gary takes a step forward to do just that every day.

Forgiving is not forgetting. They are two very different things. Gary still feels the effects of the divorce some twenty-five years later. No eraser exists that can remove all the damage or the memory of it. The pain still occasionally peeks through the sur-face. But Gary chooses each day to forgive, to set aside the past rather than forgetting it, and to spend his effort on making this day the most fruitful it can be. He doesn't forget the hurt; rather, he moves past it.

Forgiveness has been a twenty-year journey, a long process, for Gary, with small steps taken in a series of moments along the way: prayer here; Bible study there; reflection and prayer ongo-ing. No magic wipe-it-all-away moments. Just one step at a time, seeking to become the-best-version-of-himself, trusting God to fill in the gaps, and offering forgiveness to others just as he hopes to receive forgiveness for himself.

The process has worked. Gary today is at peace with him-self. He does not deny the mistakes; rather, he accepts them. He focuses on the present and what he can control now rather than continuing to relive the pain and suffering of the failures that cannot be undone. That is healthy. That is progress. And it has taken time.

With the key of forgiveness, Gary has successfully built a vibrant relationship with his children and seven grandchildren in a way that seemed unimaginable twenty years ago. Everybody needs to forgive somebody. For Gary, the first person to forgive was himself.

| | |

QUESTIONS FOR DISCUSSION

1. Name three things in your life that are journeys and processes even though you wish they could occur in a moment; for example, losing weight, dating and finding a spouse, getting in shape, earning a degree. What do these journeys teach you about the journey of forgiveness?

2. What are the key habits that will help you learn to forgive more and more over time? Gary used the keys of daily prayer, a group Bible study, and increasing generosity to cultivate a more forgiving spirit. What key habits can you use?

REAL LIFE HELP 9

Embrace the Eucharist. In the Eucharist, Jesus offers Himself to you. He places His own body and blood in you to change you. He has big hopes for your soul and for your life. He wants you to become a little Christ. That means Jesus wants you to be an extraordinary forgiver. And a great habit to grow your forgiveness over time is to receive the Eucharist as often as possible. If you do not go to Mass each Sunday, begin that habit. If you go each week, begin adding weekday Masses to your schedule to supplement the amount of Eucharist in you. Your transformation into a little Christ occurs as a process, and so does your ability to forgive. The Eucharist feeds and fuels that process.

Here's one idea to help you embrace forgiveness more deeply in the Eucharist: As you receive Communion, take time before, during, and after to gaze at the crucifix. Meditate on Jesus' divine mercy for you. Welcome that mercy into your life.

10

Seeing Beyond the Past to Believe the Best: "Jane"

*"As I looked around the crowd, I saw nothing
but puzzled faces and looks of curiosity."*

Message from a First-Century Jewish Scribe

Books—I could spend my entire day swimming in them. I've always loved to read and study, so when my father told me that I had been chosen to be a scribe, it just fit. Studying, reading, copying scrolls and books—that was me, a Jewish scribe. And getting paid to do it. I could imagine no better life. It was perfect!

I enjoyed scribe school more than most of my friends. Knowing the fine points of the law played to my strengths. I like detail and precision. Our Hebrew language studies became my passion; the Scriptures, my first love. God's law is perfect, and I was trained to share that perfection with the other Jews around me. I loved the fact that people came to me to discover God's will and His words, to help them discern right from wrong. That's what scribes do. Not to mention, as scribes we enjoyed power and respect. Prestige came with the position, and I liked that. Having the people at a restaurant give you the seat of honor, or neighbors bring gifts so they can ask your opinion—who wouldn't like that?

Plus, I got to do a lot of good. I settled marriage disputes, navigated business deals gone bad, and resolved arguments between neighbors. I interpreted the law and determined who was right and scolded who was wrong. I was a scribe, an upright man of God.

The day I met Jesus started out like any other. I was at work when I heard the clamor outside. Some men had found one of their married friends in bed with a woman. Adultery! That was my specialty. And this time, the evidence was obvious. I mean, she was practically naked right there before us. As a scribe, obviously, I knew that the sin of adultery was a highlight on God's Top Ten list. The Scriptures were clear. This woman's fate was decided; death by stoning was the only answer. In fact, the only question was whether the man should also be punished by death. We gathered our rocks and we were ready. This brazen naked lady sprawled in fear before us, vulnerable with a look of horror combined with shame etched on her face.

But before we hurled stones, Benjamin, one of the Pharisees, wanted to make a point. We were all so tired of this Jesus fellow and all the hoopla everywhere He went. "Have you seen Jesus?" "That Jesus, He's amazing." "I wonder if Jesus will come by my house today?" It really was nauseating.

His teaching seemed to dazzle everybody. Didn't folks realize that we scribes were the ones who *really* knew the Scriptures? After all, God put us in charge, didn't He? That was our job.

Anyway, Benjamin persuaded us to drag the naked woman in front of Jesus when He was teaching outside the temple. The crowd listening to Jesus was enthralled, bedazzled looks in each person's eyes. This, at last, was our chance. This time, we would expose Jesus as the fraud and impostor He was. Right there for everyone to see.

We placed that sex-filled woman right in front of Him and reminded Him of the painful facts: "In the law, Moses commanded us to stone such a woman. Now, what do you say?" We had Him. There was no being Mr. Smarty-Pants to that question. We knew we'd catch Jesus this time and bring Him to justice. For once, everyone would see who He really was: a cheap-trick artist.

Then it happened. Eerie silence. It felt like an entire afternoon passed as the silence hung in the air. I mean, it was weird. There we were, a crowd of people, a trembling naked woman, some scribes and Pharisees, and Jesus. We asked Him a simple question, and He finally bent over and started writing with His finger on the ground. What in the world is that? Writing on the ground with your finger? Is this kindergarten or something?

So Solomon, another Pharisee, kept peppering Him with questions. "You know what the law says. What do you say about that? You have heard what Moses said. What about you?" Still Jesus stayed bent over. More silence. Stonewalling, I suppose. We bombarded Him with more questions, and He said nothing. We just knew we had Him, and then He opened His mouth. He straightened up and said to us, "Let anyone among you who is without sin be the first to throw a stone at her."

Of course we had sins. Who doesn't? But, I have to admit, the man had stumped us. I started thinking about how I had worked a couple of hours on the Sabbath because I was behind with my clients, and then I remembered having looked at my neighbor's cloak last week and really wishing I had that instead of him. I couldn't get all the bad thoughts out of my head. Evidently, nobody else could either. As I looked around the crowd, I saw nothing but puzzled faces and looks of curiosity. Nobody had any idea what to do, so one by one, we dropped our rocks and walked away.

Later I heard that Jesus asked the woman, "Woman, where are they? Is there no one left to condemn you?"

She said, "No, sir."

Then, they say, Jesus said something I still cannot figure out. He looked her in the eye and said, "Then neither do I condemn you. Go your way, and do not sin again." Who was He to contradict Moses? Jesus forgave her sin. Right then, right there. I mean, she was naked and everything. And He forgave her. What do you do with that?

Jesus not only forgave her. He pointed her toward something better: "Do not sin again." It was like Jesus thought she could become a better person. He was not worried about her past. Instead, He pointed toward her future: "Go your way, and do not sin again."

Amazing. Jesus saw past her adultery to something greater.

He erased the mistake and sent her forward. There we were, ready to kill her for what *had* happened, and Jesus released her to what *could* happen: Do not sin again.

That is forgiveness. Freedom from the past. Freedom for the future.

|||

QUESTIONS FOR DISCUSSION

1. What habit or hang-up do you cling to most? An addiction? An unhealthy routine? A destructive thought pattern that you have used for years, such as anger? Or always thinking the worst about people?
2. Describe in three sentences the-best-version-of-yourself. Whom does Jesus believe you can become? What future does He point you toward?

REAL LIFE HELP 10

Remember your baptism. A simple way to embrace God's forgiveness is to think of when you were baptized. God washed away your sin. He included you as a part of His family. That means He has invited you to bring your sins, regrets, and deepest hurts to Him. Why? Because He still washes them away. Remember, you became His when you were baptized! You belong to Jesus and to His family. And that is good news.

When the priest sprinkles water on the congregation during Mass, remember that you belong to Jesus. You are baptized. When you enter or leave Mass, use the holy water to mark your forehead and remember. You have strength greater than your own. You belong to Jesus, and He believes in you.

11

Touching the Heart
of God: Corrie

*"I had never known God's love so
intensely as I did then."*

While the Nazis occupied his native Holland during World War II, Casper ten Boom ran a watchmaker's shop on the lower floor of his home in the Dutch city of Haarlem. Upstairs, his daughter Corrie emerged as the chief organizer of an underground movement to rescue Jews. Because of the ten Boom family, nearly eight hundred Jews escaped arrest and certain death at the hands of Hitler's regime. Eight hundred lives were saved.

The tall, narrow ten Boom family home featured a steep staircase up to each landing. Upstairs, in the wall of Corrie's bedroom, the ten Booms had crafted a hiding place for Jews, whom the family housed, rescuing them from the Nazi threat. They had created the hiding place just in case the secret police made a raid. In preparation for the worst, the ten Booms conducted regular evacuation drills to prepare to keep the fugitive Jews safe even in the event of an unexpected knock at the door from the Gestapo. Each member of the household lived on edge and in fear.

Finally, the raid they had always feared arrived. The date: February 28, 1944. A sudden rap at the door startled the family and their Jewish guests. Corrie feverishly hid the Jews and other members of the underground behind the wall in her room before the police could find them. Miraculously, everyone in the hiding place eventually escaped.

Sadly, however, the Gestapo arrested and imprisoned the entire ten Boom family. Casper, age eighty-four, died ten days later. Corrie and her sister, Betsie, were eventually transferred to the infamous Ravensbrück concentration camp, near Berlin, where Betsie died ten months later. A nephew, Kik, died from abuse and starvation in another camp.

Remarkably, Corrie was released from Ravensbrück through a clerical error. She quickly returned home to her native Holland, where she was determined to help those who had suffered. After the war, Corrie began receiving invitations from Christian groups in other countries asking her to speak about her inspiring experiences of rescue, courage, and survival.

As she was completing one of those talks, Corrie was stunned to see a man whom she immediately recognized as one of the feared guards she had known at Ravensbrück. Her mind immediately flashed back to her own suffering and the loss of her family. In her own words:

"One moment I saw the overcoat and the brown hat; the

next, a blue uniform and a visored cap with its skull and cross-bones. It came back with a rush: the huge room with its harsh overhead lights; the pathetic pile of dresses and shoes in the center of the floor; the shame of walking naked past this man. . . ."

Corrie's mind fixated once again on the horrors she had experienced at Ravensbrück. Now, standing years later in a place far away, she recoiled from the man, who was making his way forward. He had not merely been a Ravensbrück guard; he had been one of the cruelest guards of all.

The man threw his hand out to greet Corrie. "A fine message, fräulein! How good it is to know that, as you say, all our sins are at the bottom of the sea!"

The moment of confrontation forced Corrie to reflect on her own speech, in which she had spoken so easily of forgiveness. Forgiveness that had seemed so easy to describe now presented itself in a very difficult form right before her eyes. She fumbled in her pocketbook rather than take that outstretched, cruel hand. Anything to grab a moment to allow her heart and her mind to settle down. As she remembered her dead sister, the fear that had captivated them at the camp, and the horrors of so many people starving to death or being executed in gas showers, sheer revulsion for those who had imprisoned her washed over her, saturating her body and mind.

"He would not remember me, of course," Corrie would say later. "How could he remember one prisoner among those thousands of women? But I remembered him and the leather crop swinging from his belt. I was face-to-face with one of my captors and my blood seemed to freeze."

The guard spoke to Corrie. "You mentioned Ravensbrück in your talk. I was a guard there." And Corrie realized that he did not recognize or remember her or her family. While he had no memory of her at all, she remembered him vividly.

His words prattled out. "Since that time, I have become a Christian. I know that God has forgiven me for the cruel things I did there, but I would like to hear it from your lips as well. Fräulein, will you forgive me?"

Again, he extended his hand, reaching out to her own.

Corrie found herself sucked into a vortex of emotions and memories. "I stood there—I, whose sins had again and again been forgiven—and could not forgive. Betsie had died in that place—could he erase her slow, terrible death simply for the asking? It could not have been many seconds that he stood there, hand held out, but to me it seemed hours as I wrestled with the most difficult thing I had ever had to do."

The gravity of the moment paralyzed Corrie ten Boom. This brave woman who had risked her life so courageously now found herself incapable of responding to a man who had asked her that simple question: "Will you forgive me?"

She knew the answer, but she struggled to find the words. "For I had to do it—I knew that. The message 'God forgives' has a prior condition: that we forgive those who have injured us. 'If you do not forgive men their trespasses,' Jesus says, 'neither will your Father in heaven forgive your trespasses.'"

It was clear. Corrie not only *had* to forgive this man, she also *needed* to forgive him. For his sake and for her own. The door to a healthy future felt locked, but she knew forgiveness provided the key, if only she could muster the strength to offer it.

She said, "I knew it not only as a commandment of God, but as a daily experience. Since the end of the war I had had a home in Holland for victims of Nazi brutality. Those who were able to forgive their enemies were able also to return to the outside world and rebuild their lives, no matter what the physical scars. Those who nursed their bitterness remained invalids. It was as simple and as horrible as that."

It was almost as if God were showing her that the choice was real. Choose forgiveness and unlock your door to a new life, healing, and your future. Deny forgiveness and remain locked in the prison cell of your bitter memories that will ultimately destroy you.

Corrie reached out. "And so woodenly, mechanically, I thrust my hand into the one stretched out to me. And as I did, an incredible thing took place. The current started in my shoulder, raced down my arm, sprang into our joined hands. And then this healing warmth seemed to flood my whole being, bringing tears to my eyes."

Extending her hand, offering her heart, and sharing forgiveness, Corrie ten Boom flung open the door that had been locked for so many years.

"I forgive you, brother!" she cried. "With all my heart."

And, in the words of Corrie, "For a long moment we grasped each other's hands, the former guard and the former prisoner. I had never known God's love so intensely as I did then."

Forgiveness unlocks and opens the door precisely because at that moment we most powerfully experience the presence of God. At that moment of courage, when you reach out your hand and offer your heart, God steps in. You can almost touch Him then, simply because His heart is right there beside you.

Everybody needs to forgive somebody. In an unexpected moment, Corrie ten Boom realized that more than ever before. With no advance notice, yet saturated by grace, she forgave a man whose evils had led to her own suffering and even to the deaths of her family. Because of her courage, she came to speak a truth that can be known only when you forgive: "I had never known God's love so intensely as I did then."

| | |

QUESTIONS FOR DISCUSSION

1. At what moment in your life did you feel closest to God? At what moment in the past week did you feel closest to God?
2. Describe the most powerful moment of forgiveness you have ever experienced. Who was involved? How did forgiveness occur? How did you feel?

REAL LIFE HELP 11

Perform an act of kindness. Being kind to someone who has taken advantage of you prevents you from feeling resentful, and can also change his or her heart.

For example, in a well-known story, a Chinese Christian owned a rice paddy next to a paddy owned by a Communist. The Christian irrigated his paddy by pumping water out of a canal using a small leg-operated pump that looked like a bicycle. Every day, the man pumped enough water to fill his field. But every day, the Communist would come out, remove some boards that kept the water in the Christian's field, and let all the water flow down into his own field below. By doing that, the Communist didn't have to pump any water for himself.

This selfishness grated on the Christian. The injustice continued day after day until finally he prayed, "Lord, if this keeps up, I'm going to lose all my rice, maybe even my field. I've got a family to care for. What can I do?"

The Lord answered. The next morning the Christian arose in the predawn hours and pumped water into the lower field of his Communist neighbor. Then he replaced the boards and pumped water into his own rice paddy. In a few weeks both fields of rice were doing well. And better yet, the Communist became a Christian. Kindness overcame selfishness. Good conquered evil.

Find someone this week and do something kind. Do not announce it to anyone, and act with no expectation of being noticed or rewarded—just a pure act with a pure heart. Notice how simply doing that softens your heart.

Next week, find a way to perform a kind act for someone who has injured you. Again, no announcements or expectations. Just act kindly, and allow God to soften you. Be blessed.

Everybody needs to forgive somebody. Kindness can clear the way.

| 12 |

Creating Beauty out of Ugliness: John Paul

Even in that distressing moment, St. John Paul II has the presence of mind to recognize that sixty-four years before, something momentous occurred.

As a Methodist in 1978, I found the pope irrelevant. What did he, the leader of Catholics, have to do with me? With the election of John Paul II, my perspective changed completely.

For reasons unknown to me, I paid attention to this little Polish man who seemed so loving. As with so many other pieces of God's mosaic work in my soul, I cannot explain how the pope's holiness attracted me. But the truth was clear: Holiness emanated from John Paul II wherever he went, even when he appeared through a television screen thousands of miles away. Countless people appear on television, and not a single one communicates holiness. Yet St. John Paul II merely passed by in his vehicle, waved, or spoke a word to the crowd, and a gentle holiness emerged from the television as I watched in North America.

How could holiness translate through a television screen? I had no idea, but I knew it was real.

I was attracted to his holiness like a thirsty man to a glass of cool water.

One word describes St. John Paul II: *different*. Different from the world. Different from most Christians. Just plain different. Of course, St. John Paul II lived a life devoted to continuous prayer. Spending time in adoration before the Blessed Sacrament, seeking complete engagement and unity with God, provided the staple for his day. And that time somehow transformed him into a vessel of grace that I had never encountered before.

While I was finding my way home to the Church, a Protestant friend encouraged me to read *John Paul the Great*, Peggy Noonan's account of the events of May 13, 1981. Ironically, that friend had no idea about my journey toward becoming Catholic, nor did he know that St. John Paul II had exercised such a great influence on my soul. But he was right. That long-ago day captures the essence of John Paul II and demonstrates how forgiveness defined his holiness.

The year is 1981, and he has been pope for about two and a half years. He arrives in St. Peter's Square at 5:00 p.m. among a crowd of nearly twenty thousand people. The pope smiles, waves, holds children, and blesses them. It is a marvelous day.

Suddenly, a shot rings out, then another—shots from an automatic pistol as a Turkish prison escapee, a Muslim man named Mehmet Ali Agca, attempts to assassinate Pope John Paul II. One bullet grazes the Holy Father's elbow. The second bullet pierces his side and enters his abdomen. He falls backward, into the arms of his personal secretary, Fr. Stanislaw Dziwisz.

The Holy Father immediately begins to pray. In other words, his very first impulse in a crisis is to speak with God, showing stunning presence of mind and spirit. The pope so embodies prayer that he continues devotion even into the valley of the shadow of death. It's as if he has a prayer reflex.

Those nearest him sense that he will die. The bleeding is profuse and the damage great. As he prays, the pope realizes it is 5:00 p.m. on May 13. He has the presence of mind to remember that on this day in 1917, the Virgin Mary first appeared to the shepherd children in the field near Fatima. So, of course, the Holy Father begins to pray for the aid of Our Lady of Fatima.

Keep in mind that the pope has five abdominal wounds and the primary bullet has missed his main abdominal artery by a tenth of an inch. Even in that distressing moment, St. John Paul II has the presence of mind to recognize that sixty-four years before, something momentous occurred.

So the Holy Father prays to the Blessed Mother for help.

At five o'clock in the afternoon, the trip from St. Peter's Square to the hospital, because of traffic, averages thirty minutes. That day it takes just eight. The pope spends five hours in surgery. Everyone just knows he is going to die because the damage to his body is so horrific. Yet, St. John Paul II said later, "I had a vision that I was going to be saved."

The pope comes out of surgery, and what is the first thing he does? He asks to see the bullet. They bring him the assassin's bullet that surgeons have removed from his body. He rolls it around in his fingers and instructs his staff to take the bullet to Fatima and have it grafted there into the crown on the statue of Our Lady. You can see the bullet there still today, a gift of holiness and prayer.

Two years after the assassination attempt, Christmas of 1983 arrives. The Holy Father realizes he has never met with, nor expressed forgiveness to, his would-be assassin. So the pope, the head of the Church, goes during Christmas week to Rebibbia, the death row prison in Italy, to meet personally with Agca.

John Paul II, in his person, brings all the strands of holiness together and embodies the words of St. Paul instructing the Thessalonians: "See that none of you repays evil for evil, but always seek to do good to one another and to all" (1 Thessalonians 5:15). In other words, by moving to offer forgiveness, the pope was repaying evil with good.

Before their meeting, the pope celebrates Mass with the death row inmates. Afterward, the man who occupies the seat of Peter sits for two hours in a plastic chair with the man who tried to end his very life. The two men sit directly across from each other, the Holy Father and the would-be assassin who tried to kill him.

As they meet, the Holy Father discovers that Agca is mortally terrified of the Virgin Mary. Agca reasons that since Mary saved the pope, she will then seek to kill Agca for his crime. For two hours, St. John Paul II shares grace and love with a Muslim Turkish prison escapee. The pope explains to Agca that the Blessed Mother does not despise him but rather loves him and yearns for him to know her son, Jesus. Two men sitting in one of the darkest places on earth, death row, and for a moment, an intense concentration of the light of Christ fills the room.

Forgiveness has opened the door not of Agca's death row cell but of the prison cell of his heart. Even more remarkably, forgiveness has transformed a would-be assassin and his intended victim into friends. Everybody needs to forgive somebody, and St. John Paul II realized that truth.

From that moment onward, the pope and his assailant shared a bond. In 2005, when the Holy Father lay dying in the hospital, he received a get well card from Mehmet Ali Agca. When the pope later died, the first request the Vatican received to attend the funeral Mass was from Agca.

The pope had such impact not because of what he did, but simply because of who he was. Holiness in prayer and a heart saturated with love displayed themselves in a simple act of forgiveness, offered in a death row prison cell by the leader of 1.2 billion Catholics, a man who certainly did not *have* to forgive. Rather, he knew that he *needed* to, not just for Agca's sake but for his own.

Forgiveness changes everything. That is our destiny. Everybody needs to forgive somebody.

| | |

QUESTIONS FOR DISCUSSION

1. What do you remember most about St. John Paul II?
2. Have you ever tried to repay evil with good? Did it work or did it make the situation worse?

REAL LIFE HELP 12

Write a letter to someone who has hurt you very much. You may choose to mail it later or you may not, but writing the letter is an important first step toward your healing and the release of the power that person holds over your heart. In your letter, express the hurt you have experienced. Write it out in detail. Share with the person how you feel. Be as specific as possible. Then express that you forgive the person who has hurt you so deeply. Release him or her from any animosity or harsh feelings you may have.

Feel the burden being lifted as you write the words to offer forgiveness. It doesn't matter whether the person is willing to receive your forgiveness or even acknowledge that what he or she did was wrong. This letter gives you the chance to say things exactly as you wish to say them. Be a person of grace. Extend forgiveness even as you describe your pain. You may at some point choose to mail the letter if the person is still living and you know where he or she is. Or the letter may simply remain sealed in your desk as an expression that you needed to make. Again, the other person's response is not the important factor. Your offer of forgiveness is the key that unleashes the power of grace in your life.

Why We Call
It "Good Friday"

When you think about it, it really is remarkable that we call that day good, isn't it? Think about the details for a moment. Jesus died hanging on the cross. As He suffered, the soldiers below cast lots for His garments. Jesus looked down at them and prayed to God, "Father, forgive them, for they don't know what they're doing." These words are remarkable. As Jesus undergoes an excruciating death, humiliated before the crowd, He actually pauses and offers forgiveness. He stares into the eyes of evil, darkness, and death, and rather than cursing, Jesus unlocks the door of forgiveness right there in front of everyone. Wow.

What a glimpse of God's heart! For some reason, we call the day that He died Good Friday. Why in the world would we call it good? After all, it was a day of extraordinary suffering and death.

On Jesus' day of humiliation, He was brought before Pilate, taken by the guards, flogged, given a crown of thorns, mocked, hit in the face, and forced to carry His own cross. They scourged His body, ripping the flesh open and inflicting nearly unbearable pain. Yet He endured it.

As Jesus hung nailed to the cross, the soldiers placed a sign over His head and then they gambled for His clothes. His only drink was wine (more like vinegar) thrust in His face on a sponge. This tragedy happened to the Son of God, yet somehow we call it good?

Worse than the humiliation was the physical agony, the excruciating pain. It will come as no surprise that our word *excruciating* comes from the Latin word *excruciare*, which means "from the cross." In other words, when we describe the worst kind of pain, excruciating, we are referring to the cross of Christ itself.

And it is easy to see why the cross defines our word for the worst pain imaginable by humans. A soldier would nail the body to the cross—first the hands and wrists, then the feet. Then, several soldiers would raise the cross and drop it into a hole with a jolt that caused more pain than the nailing itself. Because of the upright position of the cross in the ground, the victim's joints dislocated and tore apart. Finally, the slow, painful process of death began. Gradually the victim's shoulders sank. From his half-kneeling position, the crucified one would try to push with his feet to become more upright, but the nails tore at his flesh. The physical collapse was inevitable. Breathing became increasingly difficult. The heart was beating rapidly because the lungs were starved for oxygen. Terrible agony followed. Excruciating.

Jesus hung on the cross fully exposed, naked to the sun and the elements, without food or drink . . . with nothing. He could die from heart failure, asphyxiation, starvation, dehydration, exposure, or any number of other causes. It was a dark day—how could anyone describe it as grand, glorious, or good? Good Friday? It really makes more sense that Germans look at this and call it Karfreitag, or Grief Friday. This day surely is more grief than good.

Jesus died for the world there on the cross. The sign nailed over His head was written in Latin, Greek, and Hebrew—the languages of the Roman Empire, the common man, and the Jew, respectively. Those languages embody that Jesus died on the cross for the entire world.

"For God so loved the world that he gave his only Son, that whoever believes in him should not perish but have eternal life." (John 3:16)

People explain His death in many ways, but there is no denying that Jesus' suffering and agony on the cross show us the evil and sinister side of human nature. We do know this: God's plan is perfect. For Jesus, it is Grief Friday, but for us, it really is Good Friday. Our sins are forgiven. We are whole and complete. Our forgiveness is real. The world flung everything imaginable at Jesus, hurling insults and vinegar in His face even as He died. And in return, Jesus used the key of forgiveness and flung open the door to heaven.

Jesus said, "Father, forgive them; for they know not what they do." (Luke 23:34)

In fact, Jesus' entire mission is forgiveness. That is because God's plan for the whole world is forgiveness and reconciliation. In a word, that is God's heart: forgiveness. And that is God's work: reconciliation. We have turned our backs on Him, and He desires to make us right. Our hearts have wandered. So Jesus comes to tell us to repent, to point the way home, and to show God's love. Finally, Jesus is willing to die on the cross to do for us what we cannot do for ourselves—to take away our sin. The truth is plain: When you look at the cross, you see the very heart of God.

We need forgiveness, and God wants to forgive. He yearns to forgive. His very heart is forgiveness. But notice also the words of Jesus as He shares the Lord's Prayer, when He teaches His disciples, "Forgive us our trespasses as we forgive those who trespass against us."

Jesus is not merely saying that we need forgiveness. We know that we do. In fact, He takes it one step further: If you are not able to forgive others, God will not forgive you. God binds Himself to the promise that just as you forgive others, He will forgive you. The more you forgive, the more you will be forgiven.

That is the basic law of the harvest and of the kingdom of God (see Galatians 6:7–8). Do you want love? Then give love away. Do you want to receive peace? Give peace away. Do you want forgiveness? Know that the more you forgive, the more forgiveness you will receive. The more you live a lifestyle of forgiving others, the less you will be affected by bitterness, grudges, and resentment. The more you give, the more you get.

When you clench your fists, fold your arms, and grit your

teeth in anger or hatred toward someone, you have no room in your heart for God to place His hand in yours. Replace your clenched fist with an open hand and watch as God fills your soul to overflowing.

The lesson is simple: Give forgiveness and you will unleash a flood of grace from heaven. Everybody needs to forgive somebody. When you do just that, you will open the door to becoming the-best-version-of-yourself as you lavish God's grace on people around you and on yourself. Best of all, you will also discover that you are touching the very heart of God.

ABOUT THE AUTHOR

Dr. Allen Hunt is a nationally known Catholic communicator, Bible teacher, and best-selling author.

He earned a Bachelor of Business Administration from Mercer University, a Master of Divinity from Emory University, and a Doctor of Philosophy in New Testament and ancient Christian origins from Yale University. He has taught at Yale Divinity School, Berry College, and the Pontifical Faculty of the Immaculate Conception at the Dominican House of Studies, in Washington, D.C.

On January 6, 2008, Allen entered the Catholic Church. This transition represented the culmination of a fifteen-year journey, which was encouraged by a group of Dominican sisters who began praying for him in 1992. Allen chronicled much of his journey in his powerful book, *Confessions of a Mega-Church Pastor: How I Discovered the Hidden Treasures of the Catholic Church*, published by Beacon Publishing.

As a speaker, Allen inspires "everyday" Catholics to more fully recognize the genius of Catholicism, the role it's meant to play in their lives, and how to share that genius with others.

His books include:

- *Nine Words: A Bible Study to Help You Become The-Best-Version-of-Yourself*

- *Life's Greatest Lesson: What I've Learned from the Happiest People I Know*
- *The 21 Undeniable Secrets of Marriage*

Allen partners with Matthew Kelly as a Senior Advisor at Dynamic Catholic. The Dynamic Catholic team is dedicated to reenergizing the Catholic Church in the United States by developing world-class resources that inspire people to rediscover the genius of Catholicism.

Allen and his wife, Anita, live in Atlanta. For more information on him and his work, please visit DrAllenHunt.com and DynamicCatholic.com.

Discussion Guide

INTRODUCTION

Books change our lives. What we read today walks and talks with us tomorrow, so in many ways we become what we read. We hope this book will change your life and the lives of the people you are gathering to discuss it with.

At Dynamic Catholic, we believe that if Catholicism is to thrive, then we as Catholics need to become continuous learners.

Spiritual reading has been a crucial part of the Catholic experience for centuries, but with the growing demands and distractions of modern life, people are reading less and less. This is tragic, because so many people have so many questions about Catholicism at this time, and unless we are feeding our minds with great Catholic thoughts, we will not be able to share our faith in a way that is articulate, bold, and inspiring.

One of our goals at Dynamic Catholic is to encourage Catholics to start reading great Catholic books. Each year we will make these books available through the Dynamic Catholic Book Program. Dioceses and parishes can purchase them for just two dollars per copy so that the books can be distributed to everyone who attends Christmas or Easter Mass.

Our strategy is very simple: Encourage every Catholic in the United States to read two great Catholic books each year. We believe this would be a game changer for the Catholic Church in this country.

We hope you enjoy *Everybody Needs to Forgive Somebody* and we pray this study guide is a useful resource as you explore what God is saying to you at this point in your spiritual journey.

May God bless you with a prayerful spirit and a peaceful heart.

The Dynamic Catholic Team

STUDY GUIDE PURPOSE AND FORMAT

The purpose of this study guide is to help readers delve further into the book by exploring personal reactions and applications. While it has been produced primarily for use in small faith groups and book clubs, it can also be used by individuals for personal reflection.

The study guide comprises six sessions. These sessions will likely take place once a week, at the discretion of the group.

Each session follows the same format:
- Opening Prayer
- Discussion Questions
- Closing Prayer
- Announcements

We recommend that a group meet for sixty to ninety minutes, but that the group agree at the outset upon a fixed length of time and adhere to that time frame.

It is assumed that participants will have completed the reading assignment before attending each session.

READING SCHEDULE

Session One (Read pages vii–15)
- Imagine
- The Weight Was Not Only Holding Me Back, It Was Breaking My Back
- Opening the Way Home: Millie

Session Two (Read pages 17–37)
- The Most Successful Failure of All Time: Peter
- Welcome The Gift: Mitch
- Freedom from a Painful Past: Maria

Session Three (Read pages 41–54)
- There's Gotta be a Better Way: Bud
- Releasing the Poison: Mother

Session Four (Read pages 55–69)
- Fix Forward: Thomas
- The First Step: Amy

Session Five (Read pages 71–84)

- A Process More Than a Moment: Gary
- Seeing Beyond the Past to Believe the Best: "Jane"

Session Six (Read pages 85–105)

- Touching the Heart of God: Corrie
- Creating Beauty Out of Ugliness: John Paul
- Closing Word: Why We Call It "Good Friday"

| SESSION ONE |

Reading: Prologue, Introduction, and Chapter 1

OPENING PRAYER

*Loving Father, open our hearts and minds
and allow us to see the beauty of our faith.
Show us what is possible and fill us with the grace, strength,
and wisdom to live all the good things
we explore here together.
Send your Spirit upon us so that we can discover your dream
for us to become the-best-version-of-ourselves, and have the
       courage to defend and celebrate this true self in every
       moment of our days.
We ask you to bless in a special way the hungry, the lonely, the
       sick, and the discouraged.
Remind us of our duty toward them and inspire us to be filled
       with a profound gratitude.
We ask all this through your Son, Jesus.
Amen.*

DISCUSSION QUESTIONS

- The prologue of *Everybody Needs to Forgive Somebody* claims
  that Jesus is all about forgiveness, and it cites a number of

examples. Which example of Jesus' focus on forgiveness speaks most to you?

- The prologue also states that the power of forgiveness is underrated and often ignored. Do you agree? Are there areas of your life where forgiveness might unleash power and healing?

- In the introduction, Allen Hunt shares his own struggles with grudge holding and forgiveness. Do you struggle as well? Are there others in your life who do?

- Why do you think so many people find forgiveness to be so difficult?

- Allen also refers in the introduction to one name for God: "home." What does it mean for God to be our "home"?

- Millie, in chapter 1, made a terrible mistake and found it hard to forgive herself. Have you ever done something so painful that you find it impossible to forgive yourself? In what part of your life do you feel trapped? What difference does Jesus bring, or might He bring, to your life?

- Millie came home. What does it mean to you to "come home"? What would it take to get there? Do you believe God is your true home?

CLOSING PRAYER

The Dynamic Catholic Prayer

Loving Father,
I invite you into my life today
and make myself available to you.
Help me to become the-best-version-of-myself
by seeking your will and becoming a living example of your love
in the world.
Open my heart to the areas of my life that need to change in
order for me to carry out the mission and experience the joy
you have imagined for my life.
Inspire me to live the Catholic faith in ways that are dynamic
and engaging.
Show me how to best get involved in the life of my parish.
Make our community hungry for best practices
and continuous learning.
Give me courage when I am afraid,
hope when I am discouraged,
and clarity in times of decision.
Teach me to enjoy uncertainty
and lead your Church to become
all you imagined it would be
for the people of our times.
Amen.

ANNOUNCEMENTS

- The reading assignment for our next gathering is chapters 2, 3, and 4.
- Let your family and friends know they can request a free copy of *Everybody Needs to Forgive Somebody* by visiting DynamicCatholic.com.
- Our next gathering will be [date, place, and time].

| SESSION TWO |

Reading: Chapters 2, 3, and 4

OPENING PRAYER

Loving Father, open our hearts and minds
and allow us to see the beauty of our faith.
Show us what is possible and fill us with the grace, strength,
and wisdom to live all the good things
we explore here together.
Send your Spirit upon us so that we can discover your dream
for us to become the-best-version-of-ourselves, and have the
*   courage to defend and celebrate this true self in every*
*   moment of our days.*
We ask you to bless in a special way the hungry, the lonely, the
*   sick, and the discouraged.*
Remind us of our duty toward them and inspire us to be filled
*   with a profound gratitude.*
We ask all this through your Son, Jesus.
Amen.

DISCUSSION QUESTIONS

- When you think of your mistakes and failures, what comes
  to mind? Divorce? A time when stubbornness cost you a relationship? Bankruptcy? Job missteps? An inability to reach an

important goal? Inadequacy as a parent? Something you wish you hadn't said? Something else?

- What inspires you most about St. Peter? How is he like you?

- Might there be areas or relationships in your life in which you are blind to hurts and barriers that have grown over the years? Mitch had no idea that his wife was bitter about the words he had shouted two years before. Examine your life for possible blind spots in relationships to see if there could be areas where forgiveness is needed.

- When Mitch's wife honestly shared the need for forgiveness in their marriage, Mitch welcomed and received her honesty as a gift. Can you think of times in your life when you have heard difficult words or news from someone you love? Did you welcome those words as a gift or did you reject them?

- Like Maria, do you carry any childhood hurts? Can you see areas of your life where those pains from the past continue to affect you and your relationships today?

- Do you think forgiving is the same as forgetting? Does it help to understand that forgiving means moving past rather than forgetting?

CLOSING PRAYER

The Dynamic Catholic Prayer

Loving Father,
I invite you into my life today
and make myself available to you.
Help me to become the-best-version-of-myself
by seeking your will and becoming a living example of your love
    in the world.
Open my heart to the areas of my life that need to change in
    order for me to carry out the mission and experience the joy
    you have imagined for my life.
Inspire me to live the Catholic faith in ways that are dynamic
    and engaging.
Show me how to best get involved in the life of my parish.
Make our community hungry for best practices
and continuous learning.
Give me courage when I am afraid,
hope when I am discouraged,
and clarity in times of decision.
Teach me to enjoy uncertainty
and lead your Church to become
all you imagined it would be
for the people of our times.
Amen.

ANNOUNCEMENTS

- The reading assignment for our next gathering is chapters 5 and 6.
- Create a forgiveness journal for yourself. Allen describes how to do this at the end of chapter 1. Spend a moment each day this week writing down the areas of your life in which you need forgiveness to spring forth.
- Our next gathering will be [date, place, and time].

| SESSION THREE |

Reading: Chapters 5 and 6

OPENING PRAYER

*Loving Father, open our hearts and minds
and allow us to see the beauty of our faith.
Show us what is possible and fill us with the grace, strength,
and wisdom to live all the good things
we explore here together.
Send your Spirit upon us so that we can discover your dream
for us to become the-best-version-of-ourselves, and have the
     courage to defend and celebrate this true self in every
     moment of our days.
We ask you to bless in a special way the hungry, the lonely, the
     sick, and the discouraged.
Remind us of our duty toward them and inspire us to be filled
     with a profound gratitude.
We ask all this through your Son, Jesus.
Amen.*

DISCUSSION QUESTIONS

- What is the most painful hurt you have ever experienced at the hands of another person?

- When you think of the person who hurt you, which comes to mind first: revenge or release? Why?

- What do you think convinced Bud Welch to release his desire for vengeance? Do you think he did the right thing?

- Have you ever known someone who was murdered? Have you been close friends with a family who has suffered the murder of a loved one? How have they handled that violent death? Have they handled it well or are they struggling to deal with the anger?

- Chapter 6 shares the story of Nelson Mandela, South Africa, and a repentant police officer. What is the most important lesson for your life from this story?

CLOSING PRAYER

The Dynamic Catholic Prayer

> *Loving Father,*
> *I invite you into my life today*
> *and make myself available to you.*
> *Help me to become the-best-version-of-myself*
> *by seeking your will and becoming a living example of your love*
> *in the world.*

Open my heart to the areas of my life that need to change in
order for me to carry out the mission and experience the joy
you have imagined for my life.
Inspire me to live the Catholic faith in ways that are dynamic
and engaging.
Show me how to best get involved in the life of my parish.
Make our community hungry for best practices
and continuous learning.
Give me courage when I am afraid,
hope when I am discouraged,
and clarity in times of decision.
Teach me to enjoy uncertainty
and lead your Church to become
all you imagined it would be
for the people of our times.
Amen.

ANNOUNCEMENTS

- The reading assignment for our next gathering is chapters 7 and 8.
- Each day this week, pray the prayer of St. Francis shared at the end of chapter 3. Make a copy of it and place it in your forgiveness journal.
- Our next gathering will be [date, place, and time].

| **SESSION FOUR** |

Reading: Chapters 7 and 8

OPENING PRAYER

*Loving Father, open our hearts and minds
and allow us to see the beauty of our faith.
Show us what is possible and fill us with the grace, strength,
and wisdom to live all the good things
we explore here together.
Send your Spirit upon us so that we can discover your dream
for us to become the-best-version-of-ourselves, and have the
    courage to defend and celebrate this true self in every
    moment of our days.
We ask you to bless in a special way the hungry, the lonely, the
    sick, and the discouraged.
Remind us of our duty toward them and inspire us to be filled
    with a profound gratitude.
We ask all this through your Son, Jesus.
Amen.*

DISCUSSION QUESTIONS

- Have you ever been falsely accused of something? Perhaps a
  friend suggested that you had been gossiping about her. Or

perhaps a business associate implied that you had been less than fair. How did that feel?

- If you could fix forward, what would you do? If you asked for God's help with that, what specifically would you ask Him to help you with?

- Who is the best forgiver in your own life? Why do you think of this person in particular?

- When has someone taken the first step to forgive you? What did you learn from that experience?

- Read the Real Life Help at the end of chapter 8. Is there anything preventing you from deciding today, "I am choosing to be a forgiver"?

CLOSING PRAYER

The Dynamic Catholic Prayer

> *Loving Father,*
> *I invite you into my life today*
> *and make myself available to you.*
> *Help me to become the-best-version-of-myself*
> *by seeking your will and becoming a living example of your love*
> *in the world.*

Open my heart to the areas of my life that need to change in
order for me to carry out the mission and experience the joy
you have imagined for my life.
Inspire me to live the Catholic faith in ways that are dynamic
and engaging.
Show me how to best get involved in the life of my parish.
Make our community hungry for best practices
and continuous learning.
Give me courage when I am afraid,
hope when I am discouraged,
and clarity in times of decision.
Teach me to enjoy uncertainty
and lead your Church to become
all you imagined it would be
for the people of our times.
Amen.

ANNOUNCEMENTS

- The reading assignment for our next gathering is chapters 9 and 10.
- This week, spend ten minutes alone in the classroom of silence with Jesus in prayer. Invite Him to help you become a forgiver. Say these words as you begin and end your silent prayer time with Jesus: "I am choosing to be a forgiver." Experience how it will change your day.
- Our next gathering will be [date, place, and time].

| SESSION FIVE |

Reading: Chapters 9 and 10

OPENING PRAYER

*Loving Father, open our hearts and minds
and allow us to see the beauty of our faith.
Show us what is possible and fill us with the grace, strength,
and wisdom to live all the good things
we explore here together.
Send your Spirit upon us so that we can discover your dream
for us to become the-best-version-of-ourselves, and have the
    courage to defend and celebrate this true self in every
    moment of our days.
We ask you to bless in a special way the hungry, the lonely, the
    sick, and the discouraged.
Remind us of our duty toward them and inspire us to be filled
    with a profound gratitude.
We ask all this through your Son, Jesus.
Amen.*

DISCUSSION QUESTIONS

- Name three things in your life that are journeys and processes even though you wish they could occur in a moment; for example, losing weight, dating and finding a spouse, getting in

shape, earning a degree, buying a house. What do these journeys teach you about forgiveness?

• What are the key habits that will help you learn to forgive
more and more over time?

• What habit or hang-up do you cling to most? An addiction?
An unhealthy routine? A destructive thought pattern that you
have used for years? Tending to think the worst of people?

• Describe in three sentences the-best-version-of-yourself. Who
does Jesus believe you can become? What future does He
point you toward?

CLOSING PRAYER

The Dynamic Catholic Prayer

> *Loving Father,*
> *I invite you into my life today*
> *and make myself available to you.*
> *Help me to become the-best-version-of-myself*
> *by seeking your will and becoming a living example of your love*
> *   in the world.*
> *Open my heart to the areas of my life that need to change in*
> *   order for me to carry out the mission and experience the joy*
> *   you have imagined for my life.*

*Inspire me to live the Catholic faith in ways that are dynamic
    and engaging.*
Show me how to best get involved in the life of my parish.
Make our community hungry for best practices
and continuous learning.
Give me courage when I am afraid,
hope when I am discouraged,
and clarity in times of decision.
Teach me to enjoy uncertainty
and lead your Church to become
all you imagined it would be
for the people of our times.
Amen.

ANNOUNCEMENTS

- The reading assignment for our next gathering is chapters 11 and 12 as well as the Closing Word.
- Go to daily Mass at least one time this week. While you are there, meditate on the crucifix and Jesus' forgiving love for you. *Eucharist* means "to thank." When you receive the body and blood of Jesus, thank Him for His forgiving love.
- Our next gathering will be [date, place, and time].

| SESSION SIX |

Reading: Chapters 11 and 12 and Closing Word

OPENING PRAYER

*Loving Father, open our hearts and minds
and allow us to see the beauty of our faith.
Show us what is possible and fill us with the grace, strength,
and wisdom to live all the good things
we explore here together.
Send your Spirit upon us so that we can discover your dream
for us to become the-best-version-of-ourselves, and have the
courage to defend and celebrate this true self in every
moment of our days.
We ask you to bless in a special way the hungry, the lonely, the
sick, and the discouraged.
Remind us of our duty toward them and inspire us to be filled
with a profound gratitude.
We ask all this through your Son, Jesus.
Amen.*

DISCUSSION QUESTIONS

- At what moment in your life did you feel closest to God? At
  what moment in the past week did you feel closest to God?

- Describe the most powerful moment of forgiveness you have ever experienced. Who was involved? How did forgiveness occur? How did you feel?

- Is the sacrament of reconciliation a regular part of your faith journey? Why or why not?

- What do you remember most about St. John Paul II?

- Have you ever tried to repay evil with good? Did it work or did it make the situation worse?

- Do you prefer the term "Good Friday" or the term "Grief Friday"? Which way of looking at the day is most helpful to you?

- Do you have any habits or customs for how you observe Good Friday in your own life or family? How are those helpful for you?

CLOSING PRAYER

The Dynamic Catholic Prayer

> *Loving Father,*
> *I invite you into my life today*
> *and make myself available to you.*

Help me to become the-best-version-of-myself
by seeking your will and becoming a living example of your love
in the world.
Open my heart to the areas of my life that need to change in
order for me to carry out the mission and experience the joy
you have imagined for my life.
Inspire me to live the Catholic faith in ways that are dynamic
and engaging.
Show me how to best get involved in the life of my parish.
Make our community hungry for best practices
and continuous learning.
Give me courage when I am afraid,
hope when I am discouraged,
and clarity in times of decision.
Teach me to enjoy uncertainty
and lead your Church to become
all you imagined it would be
for the people of our times.
Amen.

ANNOUNCEMENTS

If you enjoyed *Everybody Needs to Forgive Somebody*, the next title we would recommend for you is Matthew Kelly's *The Seven Pillars of Catholic Spirituality* (CD). After that we recommend Allen Hunt's book *Nine Words*. Both titles are available through the Dynamic Catholic Book Program at DynamicCatholic.com.

Ninety percent of Catholics don't read Catholic books. We encourage you to make spiritual reading a habit in your life and to share great Catholic books with others.

DYNAMIC CATHOLIC
INSTITUTE

[MISSION]

To re-energize the Catholic Church in America by developing world-class resources that inspire people to rediscover the genius of Catholicism.

[VISION]

To be the innovative leader in the New Evangelization helping Catholics and their parishes become the-best-version-of-themselves

Join us in re-energizing the Catholic Church.
Become a Dynamic Catholic Ambassador today!

 **DynamicCatholic.com**